*Manchester United's Golden Age*
*1903-1914*
*The Life and Times of Dick Duckworth*

DESERT ISLAND FOOTBALL HISTORIES

| Club Histories | ISBN |
| --- | --- |
| Aberdeen: A Centenary History 1903-2003 | 1-874287-57-0 |
| Aberdeen: Champions of Scotland 1954-55 | 1-874287-65-1 |
| Aberdeen: The European Era – A Complete Record | 1-874287-11-2 |
| Bristol City: The Modern Era – A Complete Record | 1-874287-28-7 |
| Bristol City: The Early Years 1894-1915 | 1-874287-74-0 |
| Cambridge United: The League Era – A Complete Record | 1-874287-32-5 |
| Cambridge United: 101 Golden Greats | 1-874287-58-9 |
| The Story of the Celtic 1888-1938 | 1-874287-15-5 |
| Chelsea: Champions of England 1954-55 | 1-874287-77-5 |
| Colchester United: Graham to Whitton – A Complete Record | 1-874287-27-9 |
| Coventry City: The Elite Era – A Complete Record | 1-874287-51-1 |
| Coventry City: An Illustrated History | 1-874287-59-7 |
| Dundee: Champions of Scotland 1961-62 | 1-874287-86-4 |
| Dundee United: Champions of Scotland 1982-83 | 1-874287-71-6 |
| History of the Everton Football Club 1878-1928 | 1-874287-14-7 |
| Halifax Town: From Ball to Lillis – A Complete Record | 1-874287-26-0 |
| Hereford United: The League Era – A Complete Record | 1-874287-18-X |
| Hereford United: The Wilderness Years 1997-2004 | 1-874287-83-X |
| Huddersfield Town: Champions of England 1923-1926 | 1-874287-88-0 |
| Ipswich Town: The Modern Era – A Complete Record | 1-874287-43-0 |
| Ipswich Town: Champions of England 1961-62 | 1-874287-63-5 |
| Kilmarnock: Champions of Scotland 1964-65 | 1-874287-87-2 |
| Luton Town: The Modern Era – A Complete Record | 1-874287-05-8 |
| Luton Town: An Illustrated History | 1-874287-37-6 |
| Manchester United's Golden Age 1903-1914: Dick Duckworth | 1-874287-80-5 |
| The Matt Busby Chronicles: Manchester United 1946-69 | 1-874287-53-8 |
| Motherwell: Champions of Scotland 1931-32 | 1-874287-73-2 |
| Norwich City: The Modern Era – A Complete Record | 1-874287-67-8 |
| Peterborough United: The Modern Era – A Complete Record | 1-874287-33-3 |
| Peterborough United: Who's Who? | 1-874287-48-1 |
| Plymouth Argyle: The Modern Era – A Complete Record | 1-874287-54-6 |
| Plymouth Argyle: 101 Golden Greats | 1-874287-64-3 |
| Plymouth Argyle: Snakes & Ladders – Promotions and Relegations | 1-874287-82-1 |
| Portsmouth: From Tindall to Ball – A Complete Record | 1-874287-25-2 |
| Portsmouth: Champions of England – 1948-49 & 1949-50 | 1-874287-38-4 |
| The Story of the Rangers 1873-1923 | 1-874287-16-3 |
| The Romance of the Wednesday 1867-1926 | 1-874287-17-1 |
| Stoke City: The Modern Era – A Complete Record | 1-874287-76-7 |
| Stoke City: 101 Golden Greats | 1-874287-55-4 |
| Potters at War: Stoke City 1939-47 | 1-874287-78-3 |
| Tottenham Hotspur: Champions of England 1950-51, 1960-61 | 1-874287-84-8 |
| West Ham: From Greenwood to Redknapp | 1-874287-19-8 |
| West Ham: The Elite Era – A Complete Record | 1-874287-31-7 |
| Wimbledon: From Southern League to Premiership | 1-874287-09-0 |
| Wimbledon: From Wembley to Selhurst | 1-874287-20-1 |
| Wimbledon: The Premiership Years | 1-874287-40-6 |
| Wrexham: The European Era – A Complete Record | 1-874287-52-X |
| **World Cup Histories** | |
| England's Quest for the World Cup – A Complete Record | 1-874287-61-9 |
| Scotland: The Quest for the World Cup – A Complete Record | 1-897850-50-6 |
| Ireland: The Quest for the World Cup – A Complete Record | 1-897850-80-8 |
| **Miscellaneous** | |
| Red Dragons in Europe – A Complete Record | 1-874287-01-5 |
| The Book of Football: A History to 1905-06 | 1-874287-13-9 |
| Football's War & Peace: The Tumultuous Season of 1946-47 | 1-874287-70-8 |

# *Manchester United's Golden Age 1903-1914*

## THE LIFE AND TIMES OF DICK DUCKWORTH

Series Editor: Clive Leatherdale

Thomas Taw

DESERT ISLAND BOOKS

First published in 2004
by
DESERT ISLAND BOOKS LIMITED
89 Park Street, Westcliff-on-Sea, Essex SS0 7PD
United Kingdom
www.desertislandbooks.com



British Library Cataloguing-in-Publication Data
A catalogue record for this book is available from the British Library

ISBN 1-874287-80-5



Printed in Great Britain
by
Biddles Ltd, King's Lynn

# CONTENTS

# Index of Illustrations

# Introduction

I was not a United fan but I cried for hours the night the Busby Babes died at Munich. Longer than for my grandad. Eleven years old, I had been in love with football about two years. I knew that what made it sadder than grandad was that United were public as well as personal. They were a team. After that night of powerful emotion it became a story, initially of personalities – who had died, who had not, and who was struggling to survive. But soon it was about the club. They needed a new team. They couldn't do it straightaway, and missed a Saturday. They needed help: other clubs sold them players; and the authorities bent the law. Ernie Taylor had already played in the FA Cup for Blackpool, but the Football Association waived their important rule restricting a player to one club in their competition. So when Manchester United reached the 1958 Cup final, Taylor was there. A new story had started.

There is nothing to compare with Munich, but United once lost another team, suddenly and prematurely, almost overnight. Manchester United grew quickly after its birth in 1902. From winning promotion in 1906 to topping the First Division in December 1913, they had a powerful, at times dominant side: Champions twice, inaugural Charity Shield holders, Cup winners. That Christmas was the watershed: nearly relegated before the First World War, they were soon afterwards, and only regained prominence after the Second World War. The disappearance of that team matched, almost to the day, the equally abrupt end to Dick Duckworth's playing career. This book therefore also tells the tragedy of United's *other* infant side.

Dick Duckworth became a professional footballer in 1903. Along with fellow half-backs Charlie Roberts and Alec Bell, and their forward stars Billy Meredith and Georgie Wall, he was the driving force behind Manchester United's success. Dick lived through a dramatic decade, 1903-14. A struggle from obscurity to triumph, through war with the football authorities, and to the brink of decline back into obscurity. Dick was there through it all, the only player who was. And he was different in another way: he was a Manchester lad, a true local hero.

Dick was a leading player in the seven years, from 1907 to 1913, known as the Golden Age of football. Golden Age because it was a time for players: managers influenced little that happened on the field. Golden Age because football flourished, all its late nineteenth century promise fulfilled in a welter of exciting matches and competitions, watched by overflowing crowds in grounds being rapidly and impressively modernised. Golden Age also means Rosy Glow. Football's growth was partly on the back of players. Clubs invested in grounds because they had contained their wage costs, or almost – the players fought back. But Golden Age mostly because it was a time before something, something that destroyed so much: the Great War. A war that killed thousands of young men contained in these pages. Spectators rather than players. The newspapers that celebrated football's popularity by documenting its vast crowds – 40,000, 60,000, 100,000 – soon reported similar numbers of daily battle casualties. Many featured in both reports.

Golden Age too because football had become a mature sport. Not that the original pioneers and founders had passed on. They were still there in the corridors of power, fighting for their interests or their vision of the game, and they were columnists in the newspapers. Often both. And as the Edwardian decade progressed, these Old Masters were joined by voices that had previously been silent – players. Players had a lot to say, about their lives, their football, their place in the sport and in society. Dick Duckworth was not a leading voice. Perhaps because he was a modest, unassuming man. Perhaps because when a Manchester United man was wanted for a column (and they often were) it was their stars, the legendary Billy Meredith and captain Charlie Roberts, that newspapers approached.

This is the public story of Dick Duckworth and Manchester United through the medium of contemporary newspapers. It is not a biography, although my interest started when I met his daughter. Ada Heywood (*née* Duckworth) knew little of her father's career: almost all she remembered was sitting in the Old Trafford stands as a girl, wedged between her father and Billy Meredith. Football was more important in her life than she realised: she was born almost exactly nine months after Manchester United's first Cup win, after her parents had been separated for weeks before the final. Otherwise her awareness was unsurprising, because she was not four when injury ended Dick's playing days. Football made more impact on his oldest child Richard, who became a pro and a manager in his own time. So I researched Dick's progress for his daughter: his extended apprenticeship, the medals and honours of his maturity, and his injuries. This research persuaded me that Dick's story provided the means of giving a wider account of football in the Golden Age.

The story was only fleetingly told in contemporary books. Newspapers were everything. They reflected the immediacy and urgency of matches of the season, or matches of the day. Dick played in Cup finals, semi-finals, quarter-finals, promotion and championship deciders. These were more than matches, they were events. Dick played in Manchester United's first match at Stamford Bridge, their first games at the remodelled White Hart Lane and Hillsborough. He played in the extraordinary circumstances of United's home grounds, at Clayton and Old Trafford. And not just in England: he participated in dramatic games in Belfast, Budapest and South Africa.

The newspapers also reflected on the issues of the day, and their underlying movement. To the realities of a footballer's life: the endless travelling; crowd criticism, even violence; to relations with teammates, referees, opponents. Newspapers were not just words. The Golden Age was on the cusp of media change; gradually photographs replaced action cartoons as the means of conveying a match. But cartoons still remained central for comment, for capturing personalities and for making links between football and a wider world. The Golden Age was a volatile time of conflict and change, and it ended in disintegration. People saw the dangers, just as they saw the snow and ice settle on United's plane at Munich. But it still happened.

THOMAS TAW
July 2004

# Acknowledgements

We all need support and I received loads from my partner Geoffrina and my children Holly, Judith, Susannah, and especially Stephen. My football team, Kenchels, kept me sane, and my friend Richard Purver kept encouraging. My editor Clive Leatherdale was an unfailingly positive force. My gratitude to the football writers of the Golden Age, whether they were uncredited reporters, or used *noms de plume* like Tramp and The Veteran, or carried big names from the past like William McGregor, or were contemporary heroes like Billy Meredith. My appreciation of the period's many cartoonists, like Fred May, Amos Ramsbotham, J Nib and especially a young Tom Webster. Some illustrations have been amended for presentational purposes. My thanks to the British Library Newspaper Library, Colindale, for giving me access to their world. And also to Ada Heywood (*née* Duckworth) for giving me a reason. Most thanks to Dick Duckworth for an exemplary inspiration.

## Dedication

To a wonderful Lady in the North Country

CHAPTER ONE

# PROLOGUE

Thursday afternoon, August 28th 1913 and perspiring Manchester United players finished their pre-season trial match, Reds versus Stripes. They were a demoralised squad. Only days before, the captain of the club's glory days, Charlie Roberts, had left the club suddenly and acrimoniously. Confidence was gone. The champions of 1908 and 1911, the Cup winners of 1909, had lost their heart, modern football's greatest half-back line – Roberts, from the north-eastern nursery of top English footballers; Alec Bell, from that other rich seam, the Scottish minefields; and Dick Duckworth, Manchester's own. All had ended the previous season in conflict: all had wanted their contribution rewarded, to have some security for the years after football. The club said no, and all were gone: 'the famous half back line which was responsible for the reputation which the club have enjoyed in recent years has been broken.'

The abilities of this formidable trio were still strong. Alec Bell joined Blackburn, who were destined to become the champions of this 1913-14 season; and 'there is little doubt that Roberts is still the best centre-half in the country'. Roberts moved to Oldham for the record transfer fee for a defender and captained them to within a point of winning the unreal 1914-15 championship. And Dick Duckworth, who had been refusing to re-sign all summer, would soon show all his old fighting qualities of speed and leadership.

It was not age but money that brought the end of Manchester United's first great team: indeed *only* successful team until the 1948 Cup winners and the Busby Babes championship side of the mid-1950s. Charlie Roberts, Alec Bell and Dick Duckworth had all been with United a decade, had already earned a benefit, and felt they deserved another. The club could not afford it. It had sunk £60,000 into the new Old Trafford stadium, a debt that became a millstone around the club's neck.

Nor was there any money for replacements. Instead of a battle-hardened heart, United had seven new tin men, a motley collection recruited from outside the Football League. Their prospects were bleak. Manchester United needed a lift.

According to tradition, United's 31 professionals were entertained after the trial by the club's directors in Moseley Hall, the palatial home of J H Davies, their moneyman and benefactor. There, a welcome surprise awaited them. Secretary-manager James John Bentley had 'come to terms' with Dick Duckworth: 'when this player entered the room he had a tremendous reception from his colleagues. Duckworth said that as a Manchester man he had no desire to play for any other club, and he believed in a player staying with his club as long as he was properly treated. Although they had lost two good players he felt convinced that if the men available would only work together and maintain the good feeling which had always existed in the past, they would have a most successful season.'

Dick was true to his word. Without any pre-season training he played with the reserves on Monday evening, at modest Stalybridge Celtic. And then straight into the first team. The United players, buoyed by the resurrection of the club's last remaining totem of success, took the First Division by storm.

Seven wins in eight matches. Twenty goals scored, only six conceded. Top of the League. United were not in decline. They had started just as in their championship years. The first victims were Sunderland, the defending champions, and Sheffield Wednesday, who had finished third the previous season. Then a run of powerful performances. Dick never lost at Stamford Bridge, and United's 'really magnificent half-backs' inspired a sound beating for Chelsea on his triumphant last appearance in London. Then United outfought a combative Spurs and frustrated a thirty-thousand Burnley crowd bent on evening up old scores: 'much has been written in praise of the Manchester United half-backs of late and that praise has been rightly deserved.'

And then Charlie Roberts returned with his new title-challenging club, Oldham. Dick Duckworth had made his United debut against Roberts and now opposed him in almost his last. Old Trafford hailed Roberts as an old hero but United's 'grand half-backs turned the tide of the match', and 'put Oldham to complete rout', 4-1.

Dick's dramatic inspiration was destined to last little further. A 3-0 win against Preston proved 'the United were a great side', but it also proved to be the last authentic appearance for Manchester's local hero. Against Middlesbrough, he was twice carried off and stayed injured for a month. He was not quite finished. Dick played his last match at a supremely symbolic moment. It was the first football day of 1914, a year that would end in catastrophic European war. Manchester United's bubble burst: they lost 1-6 at Bolton, and watched Blackburn run away with the championship. The great days of the last decade were gone, and United's decline would not be reversed until after the Second World War. Dick Duckworth's absence captured United's loss. He was not in Bolton, instead finishing his career, appropriately, at Old Trafford. Dick 'tried out' his injured knee in the reserves, and lasted twenty minutes: 'the United officials made a big mistake in including Duckworth, for he was obviously unfit, and carried off in great pain.'

It all went wrong. Dick never came back. A week later United were knocked out of the Cup by a last-minute goal. The northern giants attracted a massive crowd to Swindon, where railway wealth made Town one of the powers of the Southern League. The scorer was Harold Fleming, Dick's teammate on a pioneering FA (Football Association) tour of South Africa in 1910, and his heartbreaking late strike prompted the overflowing emotion typical in football's Golden Age: '[his teammates] nearly smothered him with caresses and spectators shouted themselves hoarse. Hats were thrown in the air, and it seemed as if everyone had taken leave of their senses.'

On the surface United were still a power, still third in the championship race, but fundamentally they were in terminal decline. To some eyes it was an effect of 'Fate, Lady of Moods'. The imagery reflected the importance football had gained in the nation's culture. For others, there was blame to be accorded. Football was both sport and business: it was in the end dependent on footballers like Dick Duckworth, and their fitness was always precarious. The critics saw United's slide as an all too predictable result of failure to reward, retain or replace the old stars; and as a consequence of their legacy to the heritage of Manchester United – the debt incurred to build Old Trafford. The team's stumble became a fall, the slide became a hurtle down the league table. The ghosts of recent triumphs, the great middle line of Duckworth, Roberts and Bell, were painfully evident in a 0-6 defeat by Aston Villa: United's 'half backs did not do the things they ought to have done'. Now 'desperately anxious', defeat by Manchester City in mid-April found United third from bottom and extraordinarily in danger of relegation.

An autographed photograph of Dick Duckworth, taken at Old Trafford, October 1910

Chapter Two

# 1903-06
# Towards the Holy Grail

Dick Duckworth went slumming when he joined Manchester United. As a 'quick and clever' forward for Newton Heath, undefeated leaders of the Manchester League, he could expect four or five thousand to watch him against the likes of Failsworth. His League debut for United in November 1903 attracted a mere thousand. Professional football in the Golden Age was a wide-ranging thing: at least five thousand men were paid to play at its different levels. But their Holy Grail was the First League. Much the same is true a century later, when we call it the Premiership.

Richard Hargreaves Duckworth was Manchester through and through. Born in Collyhurst on September 14th 1882, he lived with his parents in a cottage in Crumpsall at the bottom of Harpurhey Hill, and left school at thirteen after representing the Smedley Road Board School team.

There had been two Newton Heaths. Dick's Heathens played on the North Road ground of the original railway working pioneers; whilst the other, failed Football League club, had become Manchester United in 1902. The change was profound. Newton Heath had struggled on in the Second League, perennially short of money. The players' wages were sometimes a percentage of the gate receipts. This occasioned the apocryphal story of half-hearted players asking 'Many people in the ground?' If given a low estimate, some might say 'Oh well, I don't think I'll play today – my foot isn't right' (Green, G 1978, p.2). Alternatively there was the player paid three half-crowns who told the directors that it meant 'another Sunday in'. In other words Newton Heath's wages left him so poor he could not afford to dress his best as a respectable turn-of-the-century man. He explained that his best suit was in hock for fifteen shillings and could not be redeemed even with several weeks' wages. The directors relented, gave him enough to redeem his Sunday suit, and another two shillings for 'spending brass'.

By February 1902 this hand-to-mouth existence was unsustainable. Contractors that had refurbished their stadium, Clayton, moved for bankruptcy against Newton Heath Football Club, which was £2,670 in debt. Famously, at a despairing shareholders' meeting a month later, long-standing captain Harry Stafford rose to produce a saviour – J H Davies, a self-made millionaire who headed the Pomfray and Walker Brewery. Davies had had no interest in football, and the stories explaining his involvement either describe an unlikely series of coincidences linking the two men, or, equally unlikely in 1902, suggest Stafford persuaded Davies of the club's potential as a money-making proposition in an international context.

Nevertheless, Davies was both a clever pragmatist and someone with 'an unerring eye for the potential of long-term investment'. A man who lived in princely fashion, Davies conferred his hospitality upon his staff, and thus produced a generally collegiate morale. The renaming of 'Manchester United' was not his idea, and initially did not 'meet the views of the meeting'. But by April 1902, 'the new name was a novelty ... likely to catch on.'

United or otherwise, Davies knew the club would only make money in the First League, and signalled his ambition by putting £3,000 at Stafford's disposal to find new players (Green, G 1978, p.282). Mostly experienced men. John Hope Peddie had been 'as highly praised as roundly abused' in clubs from Glasgow through Newcastle to Plymouth. Many came with credentials. Tommy Arkesden played in the 1899 Cup final. Goalkeeper John William Sutcliffe had been a double rugby and soccer international. 'Ching' Morrison had seven caps for Ireland. Billy McCartney had opposed Morrison for Scotland in the spring of 1902: the capture from Hibernians was the most notable of a small army of established Scottish imports, three of whom had the name Robertson. But less exalted prospects were not neglected. Harry Stafford, in white hat and gaudy waistcoat, could play the dandified patrician. In Ayrshire Stafford entered the lowly cot of Alec Bell's family. A sovereign was tactically dropped on the floor and the 'guid wife' of the household hastened to retrieve and return it to the Saxon visitor. Stafford disdained the coin and indicated the new wealth behind his expedition: 'Oh, don't mind, give it to the baby.' United's weekly wage bill jumped to £102. Not that Alec had any illusions: he expected to be back home in three months – after all he had never owned a pair of pumps in his life.

**1903-04**

The new United failed to challenge for promotion in 1902-03 and secretary James West was sacked, blaming his demise on the 'failure of the newer members of the club to sustain their high reputation'. Billy McCartney, for example, played only an unlucky thirteen games. The new secretary-manager, Ernest Mangnall, came from Burnley and quickly recruited local men – a couple each from Ashton Town and Newton

Heath (Dick cost a £50 'gift'). It meant personal change for the young pros: Dick Duckworth's trade was a moulder. 1903 was a time of economic depression, and in comparison with an uncertain industrial outlook Manchester United may have seemed 'a soft bed to lie upon'. But there was little time to relax. Rivals Manchester City were challenging for Manchester's first championship whilst, as early as November, United's chance of promotion to that First League already seemed gone. Preston and Woolwich Arsenal were running away with the Second League and United were in mid-table after losing to the leaders: 'it was a dreary place to be in, was Clayton, after the North End game, and the crowd leaving the United enclosure wore such a look of abject misery, despair, disappointment etc. that it added considerably to the unpleasantness of the inclement weather.'

The club had occupied its north Manchester ground at Bank Lane for a decade and although Davies immediately began investing in its fabric, Clayton's reputation suffered from two profound deficits. It was for most of each winter a 'muddy waste', made worse for players and spectators by the frequent presence on the nostrils of noxious chemical fumes. For the ground lay windward of a thirty-strong army of chimney stacks from chemical works, soapwork vats and others besides, and which overlay everything and anyone within the vicinity with an unholy concoction:

'As Satan was flying over Clayton for Hell,
He was chained in the breeze, likewise the smell,
Quoth he: 'I'm not sure in what country I roam,
But I'm sure by the smell that I'm not far from home.'

Twenty thousand watched the Preston match; the subsequent disappointment meant there were only eight thousand a few weeks later when according to the record books Dick Duckworth made his League debut. But in fact Dick had already played four significant matches. In November, United's reserves took on Glossop's full Second League side. Six thousand were attracted to Clayton, an 'interest centred to a very great extent in the appearance of three new locals on our side ... They all came out of the ordeal very well' and when Dick, at centre-forward, scored the equaliser it was no more than they deserved. Next, United killed two birds with one match. They played Ashton as part of their transfer fee for two players. Part of the proceeds also went to the Manchester and Salford Lifeboat Fund, a community gesture solidified when a 'real live MP' kicked off. One of Dick's new teammates, Alec Bell, received a sadder recognition: his father had died and 'out of respect the United turned out in new black and white jerseys'. Duckworth and Wilkinson, 'the two Newton Heath lads, both scored goals and added to their reputations, and I should not be surprised to find either of them in the first team before long.'

It was an opportune time to shine: disillusionment with the team's failure to build on the prosperity of its new owner by challenging for promotion meant newspaper hyperbole – 'drastic changes' were needed. 'Discontent has been given full vent in this last week or so regarding the state of affairs at Clayton, for the position of the club is gradually getting worse and worse, and where it will end is hard to say.' So at Grimsby, on November 28th 1903, Dick Duckworth made his first appearance in Manchester United's League team. It was an inauspicious start. As befits recent failures and Dick's own initial promise he was part of a well shuffled forward line, but not one calculated to be a 'best arrangement'. Dick was centre-forward but the attack featured four players whose acknowledged position was … centre-forward. Dick's direct opponent was someone he was destined to know very well – Charlie Roberts. The Grimsby population were unimpressed, and barely a thousand people turned up. Town were leading 2-1 when the referee called the players off, as 'it was too dark to see properly'. Earlier he had had to consult both linesmen before awarding a Grimsby goal. Fortunately for United goalkeeper Harry Moger it was so dark that the referee missed what the reporter glimpsed through the gloom – Moger fighting with a Grimsby player just before the premature end.

Dick himself emerged briefly out of a different gloom the following week, on his home debut: 'loud cheers were given as Duckworth was seen travelling towards the opposing goal, but his shot was cleverly spoiled.' But when the fog became too thick to continue it proved United's hollow salvation: 'we are only able to escape the disgrace of defeat at the hands of Leicester Fosse on our own ground, by the intervention of the elements.' Dick made his mark when he gave United an undeserved lead, but United's 'forwards were, I think, worse than ever, and only Duckworth and Sandy Robertson played anything like decently'. So Dick had made two league starts, but no finishes.

United then immediately embarked on a tough series of four matches in an English Cup-tie with Small Heath (later Birmingham City) – one 'rough and scrambling ding-dong battle' after another. The original match was tough enough, but in the first replay their opponents' captain was sorely provoked – 'Walter Wigmore [*aka* The Nasty Lump] appears to have been badly used, his jersey being partially torn from his back' – and was ordered off for kicking United's Billy Grassam in retaliation. Then

United's right-half Alec Downie was injured, and left the field: it 'rendered him about useless when he returned. Before the close he again had to seek the shelter of the dressing room.' Dick was reserve; maybe not yet ready for such rumbustious affairs, although his absence was noted: 'it was a surprise to many people not to find Duckworth in the team again, as he was without doubt our best forward against Leicester the week previous, but for some reason or other – to the outsider inexplicable – he was placed on reserve.'

Dick was now living the life of a professional footballer. For two decades top clubs had taken their players away in the 'manner of prize-fighters'. This refuge from ordinary life demonstrated a club's wealth, and the depth of their desire to succeed. It was designed to impress everyone, not least the players: 'some professionals feel aggrieved if they are not sent away. Some imagine that the game cannot be of importance because the directors do not think it big enough to send them away.' At this time Manchester City spent £1,500, eleven per cent of their income, on travelling and hotel expenses on their way to the Cup final and still made a profit of £2,250 – Second Division Preston spent only £554.

United had to match City's ambitions. The preliminary English Cup-ties were sufficiently important for the players to retire to Lytham St Annes for the original Small Heath tie. They returned to prepare for the replay in Birmingham, and yet again before a third drawn game, after extra-time, in Sheffield. Dick's colleague Bob Bonthron also demonstrated the new professionalism expected of him – indeed the ultimate professional foul was needed to save the day: 'Bonthron, one of the Manchester backs, caught and threw the ball away as his goalkeeper was sprawling on the ground. This is one of those occasions when the penalty is inadequate. A goal ought to be awarded without a doubt.'

The tie spanned seven hours on four grounds. Dick was now fully immersed in a life in which individuals and team were lauded to the skies one week, and damned the next. He had one more spot in the limelight, and then would disappear. For in between this epic series of Cup-ties United had to fulfil a league fixture, with Gainsborough Trinity, and with Alec Downie still hurt, they lacked a right-half. 'It was only five minutes before the men turned out that the side was finally decided upon,' and the right-half position was occupied by the promising young forward Dick Duckworth.

At last, without fog and darkness, Dick took his place in League records: 'Duckworth was conspicuous with good defensive play, and an accurate pass which set the home front rank once more on the move.' Dick's positive approach reaped dividends in a 'rousing struggle, full of life and excitement, and one that was anybody's game up to the finish'. United led 2-0, Trinity fought back to equalise and United pulled away again, 4-2. 'Downie was not so missed, for Duckworth made a most useful substitute, and again showed what a promising young player he is.'

Nevertheless Dick's first chance of establishing himself had gone for the moment. Alec Downie continued to be absent but United chose the slightly more experienced Alec Bell rather than his equally promising rival: 'I don't know why Bell was put in with Duckworth available for he is undoubtedly a centre half, and does not get through the same amount of work on the wing.'

Back in the reserves, Dick was showing good judgement in a series of fast and exciting matches. His teammates included other young hopefuls. There was Charlie Wright, whose transfer occasioned the friendly with Ashton; Private Daker from the Army; Jacobelli, from Manchester's Italian quarter; and little Proctor Hall who 'improves every time he turns out, and it is a great pity he is light, for he is full of purpose, and both passes and shoots well and accurately'. Dick went backwards in the queue. He did not play again for the first team, whereas Hall played eight league games, and Dick's fellow former Heathen, Harry Wilkinson, played seven. This was all the more disappointing as United's current first-teamers did not seem to match up to their new owner's First League ambitions: 'a club that will be worked up into that Division sooner or later if money and influence can do it.'

Were the current squad capable of realising these ambitions? 'I hardly think they are.' But within weeks United had revived the city's enthusiasm, and temporarily took the limelight away from rampant City, attracting a 'monstre' [sic] crowd of fifty thousand to the crucial promotion battle with Woolwich Arsenal: 'excitement has pervaded Cottonopolis all week, for the advent of the Arsenal has been long and patiently waited for.' Clayton's facilities were tested to the utmost – and the superstition of journalists just a little:

'[Olympian] passed three funerals and saw a flag at half-mast, and naturally wondered if it could be taken as a kind of omen! As for the scene on the ground, it reminded one of a Crystal Palace final. The stands were packed like herring barrels, spectators were even stowed away in the curling frames of the ironwork, and mind you this was only a Second Division gathering. What if United were in the First League next season.'

Dick stayed on the fringes as United's established right-half reasserted himself: 'To Downie, I should say belong the greatest honours.' United beat Arsenal 1-0, to creep a little nearer 'the "happy land" of our ambitions'. They had 'done wonders … We have a rare, hard-working team together now, and nothing seems to come amiss to them. They are being carried forward by an irresistible wave of success.'

But United's run of eighteen games without defeat came disastrously to an end as Sheffield Wednesday beat them 6-0 in the Cup. The camp were in mourning. '"Tis with horrible mien and very much depressed spirits … The great calamity which befel our team.' Two days later their followers expressed their anger: 'unsportsmanlike spectators … seriously troubled by the result at Sheffield, proceeded to jeer and otherwise act in a manner which neither did themselves credit nor did the players any good.' Worse, United's high-falutin' ways rendered them even more vulnerable when things went wrong, and their promotion hopes were hit by defeat at the bottom club: 'the expense incurred in special training, extra hotel bills, and all the rest of the items incidental to their stay at Morecambe have been useless, and to all intents and purposes, thrown away.'

Nevertheless, the never-say-die United camp remained 'agog with excitement' until the end, and the end came on the Monday after the Cup final: 'To be or not to be.' Not to be. Again the imagery was unfortunate. Manchester City had just won the Cup by beating Bolton Wanderers, the same Bolton that ended Manchester United's dream of promotion. Instead, Woolwich Arsenal became the first southern club in the First League.

Passionate Shakespearean prima donnas featured in United's last game, a replay of one of those matches that Dick played in and was postponed. Trouble followed the referee awarding United a goal – Leicester responded petulantly: 'to see three or four "men" lay down on the ground, apparently refusing to play, and thereby stopping everybody else from doing so, just because a goal was given against them, is, to say the least, ridiculous … All Fosse protested, Mr Bye with some difficulty extracting himself from the crowd of players which surrounded him. Then, because they could not have their own way, three of the players sat or lay down on the ground, and even when approached by the referee, they retained their positions and argued. When the game resumed, thc Fosse went wild.'

United had already made a move that would bring rich dividends. Chairman J J Bentley later complained that they delayed getting twenty-year-old Charlie Roberts until their promotion chance had gone. Nevertheless Manchester United had to beat a whole tranche of First League clubs to sign Roberts in the 'mysterious dark hours' (Green, G 1978, p.216) for a record fee of approximately £650. It was on the eve of the 1904 Cup final that demonstrated how far United were still behind the finalists, who were their close rivals Manchester City and Bolton Wanderers. Manchester United themselves were already condemned to play another season in the lower league. J J Bentley and Mr Bellows the Grimsby chairman were at the Holborn Restaurant prior to going to the Crystal Palace next day: Harry Stafford and Charlie Roberts were on the end of the phone in Grimsby. When the deal was done a special messenger rushed in the registration forms, and Stafford and Roberts raced to Manchester for that afternoon's match.

Somehow the United had captured the highly talented Roberts in the face of competition from a host of top clubs, led by the imminent Cup winners and League runners-up Manchester City. How? City's willingness to make illegal payments in this period would be exposed in 1904 and, disastrously, in 1906, so Roberts would not have lacked incentive to join football's premier clubs. United would have to better that.

Indeed that same month Manchester City signed forward Irvine Thornley from Glossop for a fee described as between £500 and £800. Thornley was one of the most promising young players around and like Charlie Roberts went on to represent England. But not before he survived various scandals over illegal payments. Thornley's agent, and father, publicly informed the many interested clubs that he would want more than the official maximum wage of £4. Eventually Mr Thornley senior, a retired butcher, received half of City's fee, and proclaimed himself an ace agent – '[he] was the man to find places for players.' The FA promptly banned him from football. It indicated City's willingness to bend the rules. But they did not get Charlie Roberts.

United's histories make no mention of a bounty from J H Davies. Roberts apparently chose Manchester United because that was the team he wanted to play for. A north-east lad from Darlington opted for a Second League club of two years duration rather than the Cup winners and nearly champions of the First League with a proven record of paying illegal inducements. Unlikely. Whatever the reason, the signing was inspired, and Roberts would prove the 'guiding star' (Green, G 1978, p.216), 'the man,' the rock on which Manchester United's success, and Dick Duckworth's career, was founded for the next nine seasons. Whatever the reason, Roberts' personal choice had a visible consequence: he became well known for his 'pallid appearance', the result of too many games in the 'insalubrious environment of Clayton's manufacturies'.

**1904-05**

Dick Duckworth talked up his prospects for his second season as a professional: '[Downie's] capable substitute is Duckworth, who says he is not going to be easily kept out of the first team.' Sadly that was what happened: the impact Dick hoped for proved elusive. As in the previous year the promotion candidates quickly detached themselves from the rest: last year's losing Cup finalists Bolton, and last year's surprise relegated club Liverpool. Manchester United failed their first hurdle in September. 'By every means of locomotion the crowds wended their way' to Clayton for Wanderers' visit, but United lost, and depression took an early hold: 'a gloom that was almost impenetrable ... The utmost desolation when the closing stages of a hard game were reached ... [the club's] only consolation being that that they reaped in liberally the shekels' of the multitude.' The informal market fared worse, the purveyors of the fashionable funeral cards being left with 'unmarketable commodities' after Bolton's unexpected victory. One United poet invested his bitterness into an elegy:

> 'Over United's tomb with silent grief oppressed,
> Claytonians mourn their heroes now at rest,
> And their bright hopes for once we overcast,
> By gallant Bolton Wanderers, conquerors at last.'

Not that United lacked fight: full-back Bonthron was his usual combative self and Bolton reacted. 'Subject to such scant courtesy, the Wanderers retaliated, and the players took liberties ... There were a good half dozen men on the field who overstepped the bounds of legitimate warfare.'

The Bolton defeat caused a rethink. It did not let in Dick, but it was Alec Bell's turn. Sandy Robertson, his experienced predecessor, was hailed as knowing all the tricks of the trade, but was no longer quick enough. Bell took over as left-half, and stayed there for nine hard seasons. Dick's own chance came a month later, in brilliant weather at Leicester Fosse. United were already trailing badly in sixth place. Alec Downie was missing with influenza and the half-back line of Duckworth, Roberts and Bell made its first appearance. They achieved a 'very clever victory', 3-0, and Dick's performance reminded commentators of his rare form last year: 'now he has got into the team Downie might find it difficult to get back.' But it was not to be, not yet.

Dick went back into the reserves. The first team enjoyed great success and were rewarded with a settled team. Even when United had nine men out injured, and five others playing crocked, Downie stayed 'in the pink' and Dick stayed in the reserves. In eight successive matches United did not concede a goal, a triumphal procession culminating in defeat of their promotion rivals. After Christmas, 40,000 – 'never was such a crowd seen at a football match in Bolton' – paid well over a thousand pounds to see United win 4-2. 'At Victoria Station I began to wonder where they all came from' as Cottonopolis folk 'bearded the lion in his den'. On the sight of what was to be the terrible crowd disaster of 1946, some neutrals from wildest Lancashire found it impossible to see … 'aw geet wedged i' a corner an' couldn't stir. Aw wur noather in nor eawt, and wur as fast as a thief, wi't tornsteel shoved i' mi belly.' Another managed to get in to the relatively sheltered enclosure but 'wor feign to scramble oght ageean'. He paid his shilling 'beawt seein' onythin' o't gam.'

United enjoyed fourteen consecutive wins and a goal difference of 43-7: 'they are indeed a great team … Words are inadequate to express the pleasure one feels.' Yet they were still anxious: 'the slightest slip means disaster.' Manchester were sitting pretty in second place, having gathered an impressive 37 points from 21 games – behind Bolton, but four ahead of Liverpool – 'our chance is the best of the bunch'. But now United hit trouble in their quest to finish in the coveted top two positions.

They lost their first league match in five months, and fell six points behind Bolton. By now, young Roberts was 'in a class by himself', but his international recognition created problems as the League season came to its climax. Roberts was first picked for England and then, controversially, for the Football League. The difficulty was that his club had to play vital league games without him, and the replacements were not successful. Meanwhile Dick Duckworth was being wasted. In a reserve team coming unstuck, Dick was doing 'splendid work, and is, in my opinion, a fine player spoiling, for his efforts are usually nullified by someone else's faults'.

It seemed significant therefore that in a Manchester Cup-tie Dick was tried in Roberts' position: 'one thing I was glad to see, and that the officials had given Duckworth a trial at centre half, and that he had done himself justice. He is a useful lad, and knows how to shoot.' Dick seemed about to emerge from his obscurity, either standing in for Roberts, or at right-half, as his main rival was feeling the effects of a hard season. 'Downie was not so effective as of old. See to it, Alec.'

But yet again, Dick had to wait. United lost further ground in the promotion race with veteran Billy Griffiths playing instead of Charlie Roberts. Griffiths now carried the disadvantage of 'added corpulence', which was unfortunate: 'I don't think anyone ever dreamed that Griffiths would be called on. Had the selection gone by merit, nothing could have kept Duckworth out of the team. The latter has one fault, I know – he won't head the ball – but he is not the first half back we have had with this failing.'

If Dick's progress was frustrating and uncertain, other footballers burst on the scene, apparently ready-made. Whilst Dick fumed in the shadow of corpulent Griffiths, those destined to be his distinguished contemporaries forged ahead. Andrew Ducat, nineteen, later one of his rivals for the England right-half position, scored a debutant hat-trick at centre-forward for Woolwich Arsenal. Another teenage, and more long-standing, centre-forward Albert Shepherd had gone from strength to strength since he opposed Dick for Bolton reserves – fifteen goals in eight reserve games, then a decisive addition to Wanderers' promotion challenge. Eight goals in his first six matches, and then ... Bolton's two matches against United were not the only ones to capture the city's imagination. The second round of the Cup saw a re-run of the 1904 final, and Wanderers felt they could exact revenge for Billy Meredith's offside goal in Crystal Palace the previous April. 'Never has [Hyde Road] held so many people,' up to 40,000; never a match which 'stirred the vitals of ... two neighbouring towns so furiously.' A cinematography presence indicated more than local interest, and many of those present would have needed to attend the cinema to see anything:

'Lads began to be belched forth from dense corners ... A man was scaling impossible heights, fell, and hurt himself. To pack the open Galloway stands, the lower range of folk rushed up as though storming Port Arthur, beaten only to return, and eventually find lodgement. Some of the spectators were fired into the enclosure most dangerously.'

At 1-1, time running out, Albert Shepherd made his name. He got the ball, dribbled fast towards goal past City defenders and unleashed the winning shot, 'the goal of a lifetime, and will be talked about for years to come.' Within one year, 'Shepherd is the best professional centre forward I have ever seen play for England.'

Billy Griffiths and not Dick Duckworth stood in for Charlie Roberts on England duty, and Burnley beat them. Dark thoughts overtook the United following: why did Roberts have to represent the honour of the Football League, when another centre-half might have been chosen from a club uninvolved in a battle for League honours? And how come promotion rivals Liverpool could refuse permission for two of their players to play in the Scottish international trial? And how could a small, struggling club like Burnley afford 'such a luxury' as to take the team away to the seaside for three days before tackling United? Some said that promotion rivals Bolton and Liverpool paid Burnley's expenses.

The Burnley 'defeat meant practically the extinction of their hopes', and United's following did not just blame outside forces: 'must one conclude that we are to be disappointed in the end ... Such thoughts ... have almost obliterated all hopes and kindly feelings towards the United team.' All three challengers had now played 26 games, with eight to go, and United trailed by three.

Then, unexpectedly, came Dick's chance. Many other hopefuls had come and gone, and now he was given only his third League game in eighteen months as a professional. Most surprisingly, it was in his original position of centre-forward. Captain Peddie was left out, and 'there was some nice passing between Duckworth and Allan, and when the latter centred for Duckworth to score the crowd cheered heartily'. But the referee gave offside, and United still trailed at home whilst Liverpool were winning 6-1. Dick gave his all – 'a supreme effort by Duckworth ended in him being slightly hurt' – then he 'shot hard, the ball grazing the post'. Jack Allan got the equaliser, and in the second half Dick Duckworth the winner, unleashing a shot which 'Spendiff was helpless to save'. It was not all good. Dick was entrusted with a penalty, and missed, to his 'evident disappointment and the chagrin of the crowd'. In United's next fixture, Dick tested Blackpool's goalkeeper 'very deceptively by an overhead kick' and then set up the only goal. United were now gloating, for their victory coincided with defeats for their rivals. Now they had all played 28 games, six to go, and Bolton and Liverpool had 47 points, Manchester United 46.

Dick had done 'excellent work in the centre', adding to his reputation, but had also transformed the team's demeanour – he had 'infused a lot of dash and fire to our front rank'. Doncaster were next: a 'rare good goal at close quarters', another with a good shot, and then a third after 'feinting for position' and hitting a shot which 'would have beaten almost any custodian. It was a beauty, and deserved the loud applause.' A first half hat-trick in only his fifth league game ever, a 6-0 win: 'the inclusion of Duckworth has brought about this excellent improvement' in prospects – 'our front rank was great'. Duckworth-inspired United were suddenly top of the league: all three clubs had 48 points from 29 games. In other words all three had only lost ten points all season, mostly to each other.

Then Dick found it was not always as easy. Next week, whilst Liverpool were winning 8-1, Manchester United were held to a goalless draw at Gainsborough Trinity, and 'for once in a way Duckworth was all at "sea".' He 'made an awful mess of a good opening', although 'he was not the only sinner in front of goal, all the others missing glorious chances'. Gainsborough then evoked dark suspicions when they next lost at home to Bolton Wanderers. United were surprised, to say the least, when it transpired that just before the game Bolton promptly closed negotiations with Trinity over their amount of compensation for the original postponement. To aggrieved, perhaps paranoid Reds, it seemed Wanderers had 'bought' the game for £80.

'We are now a point behind,' but United's determination was sharpened: 'not less than 6-0 today,' said one of our players to me as he left the dressing-room to meet the United from Beer town.' Fifteen thousand watched in cricket-weather as Manchester's United were almost as good as their word – 5-0 against Burton's, with Dick scoring two more goals. 5-0, two goals, but still below expectations. It was backlash-time: 'I have had a very big opinion of Duckworth's ability, and have watched his rise with pleasure, but he is losing valuable ground by his present form. He did not shoot often enough, and some of his passes were wild and ill-placed, while he often enough lost chances by his slowness in gathering the ball.' Unsurprisingly, if this was an influential view, Dick was left out on Good Friday, and Chesterfield's subsequent victory was a 'great blow'. Suddenly, the bubble had burst, it was the 'end of our dreams'. 'Clayton folk are not in the best of humours just now … The chance of our being certain of promotion has been thrown away.'

Two games to go, and now three points behind. The next day's match at Anfield was always going to be the decider, but now United needed to win to have any sort of chance. Liverpool could hardly believe the news from the town of the crooked spire contained in their Saturday morning paper – Chesterfield Town 2, Manchester United 0. 'At breakfast table, certain of the Liverpool management lost their usual dignified bearing, and danced for joy in a somewhat unorthodox fashion.'

All three challengers had already eclipsed the 50-points total of the 1904 champions. Into its final stages an unprecedented Second League promotion battle maintained its grip on the public. Bolton were at sedate Blackpool, where Wanderers' journalist The Tramp found himself out in the cold. An 'unprecedented crush' caused by excursioners from Bolton to the seaside evicted him from the press box 'to squat inside the playing portion of the ground, and once I was unceremoniously upset by a "muddied oaf" coming at me with a headlong charge … gently urged in my direction by what some folk would scarcely call a fair charge.'

At Anfield a similarly raucous crowd of 30,000 had far-reaching consequences. It convinced Liverpool that the club needed to develop the ground to exploit the growing demand for football's big games: 'thousands were turned hungry away. Hundreds tried to squeeze through the Press entrance, which is fixed half-way along a narrow entry … Enthusiasts in their tens were vainly offering shillings to adjoining households for a space in their windows to peep over the stand roof.' Others climbed onto roofs and towers within the ground, and several times the match was halted when hundreds were forced onto the playing field. At first there was 'nothing to choose' between the teams, and 'play was waged at a terrific pace, and the recent game with Bolton simply paled by comparison'. Then Liverpool's England international Sam Raybould completed a hat-trick. United's attack, including Dick, were 'fairly bottled up … Peddie and Co. were slow, stupid schoolboys.'

How to make sense of a second year of being so near but so far? The bitter-sweet tendency was to blame the success of their brightest star, Charlie Roberts. Roberts had just become the first Second League player to play in all three England internationals, as well as that notorious Football League representative match. Five vital points were dropped during his absences. Yes, that was the reason – 'We paid dearly for your "caps", Charlie.'

Thereafter it was partly the other way round, and Charlie Roberts never played for England again.

There was a small compensation for Dick. Alec Downie, walking painfully with the help of a stick, bemoaned his loss of a place in the Manchester United team which beat *Blackpool* to win the Manchester Cup – Dick Duckworth was at right-half, and won his first medal.

### The Summer of 1905

And then tantalisingly United glimpsed a prospect of gaining the promotion that had so frustrated Dick and the team. The summer of 1905 presented the possibility of a new and unexpected route into the First League. C E Sutcliffe proposed that the Football League be increased from 36 to 40 clubs, twenty in each division. One interested group was thought unlikely to support the change. With 34 league games already, English Cup-ties that went to three or four matches with extra time, County cups, city cups, football was already demanding enough: 'four more games will not be looked upon favourably by the players.' But the players had no say.

Essentially Sutcliffe's supporters had to persuade the Second League members to agree the change, and why should they? An increase to twenty reduced each individual club's chance of promotion. In addition, currently their only southern member was Bristol City, and all the northern and midland clubs lost money on that away fixture. Among the favourites to enter an extended League were the newly formed Chelsea and Clapton Orient, which meant increased travel and accommodation costs. The Second League tried to negotiate: Bradford City proposed that three clubs should be promoted, rather than two, to compensate for the extension. But they were outmanoeuvred. Sutcliffe resisted connection between the two proposals and crucially, ensured his came first. So the extension was agreed, and three-up, three-down was rejected.

All that remained was to decide which two teams would make up the First League from eighteen to twenty. Manchester United had reason for confidence: in the epic battle for promotion they had proved far superior to the rest of the Second League. United's Chairman, J J Bentley, was also the League President, and thus could not have been better connected. He and manager Ernest Mangnall, fortified by a salary increase to £5 a week, lobbied in United's cause.

But in vain: the vote restored both relegated teams, and left United out in the cold. Why? Some blamed Manchester City, said to have issued a circular against their neighbours. Some blamed J J Bentley, because the President of the Football League should 'owe official allegiance to no particular club'. Suspicion about Bentley's combined roles focused on his control of selecting referees, and memory of one or two decisions that went United's way. Complaints had surfaced during that spring's intense and controversial promotion race: 'What would [J J Bentley] think if in such circumstances Liverpool were credibly reported to have benefited to the extent of two points in two games which could be quoted as instances.' It was not that Bentley was accused of pressurising officials: it was just that referees are 'prone to remember whence appointments came'. Others attributed United's failure to a more prosaic cause: the rest of the Second League wanted at least one more season of good gates from a club with greater prosperity and ambition than most of the First League.

And that it would be only one more season in the Second League was 'taken for granted'. United had finished eleven points ahead of fourth-placed Bristol City. Their chances were enhanced by an absence of relegated sides, to bring First League experience and quality to compete with United. In fact, four of the League were new to this level and, in Chelsea's case, any level. Everything was set for Manchester United to dominate.

Dick Duckworth's position was more equivocal. He had made an impact, transforming a downhearted side. He scored the winner in his first match, set up the only goal in the second, achieved the hat-trick in his third and two goals in his fifth. More, he had infused 'dash' into the whole side. But he was not the finished article, and eventually failed to rise to expectations. First criticised, then dropped, he came back to suffer his first League defeat, at Liverpool – a crushing, demoralising defeat. Six goals in six matches as a forward, but in previews of the coming season, Dick went unmentioned. He would soon have to deliver. He had now been a professional for almost two full years, and had less than a dozen senior outings. All the other young players who had joined at the same time as Dick had now gone, and a new generation was being recruited. Indeed, of the teammates in his official debut match in December 1903 only one started the 1905-06 season. And yet his chances were lessened through Manchester United's booty in the summer sales: three new inside-forwards, including tall, slim Charlie Sagar who had twice won the Cup, and twice played for England.

**1905-06**

So Dick's prospects were bleak: he was once again the reserve right-half, and Alec Downie was once again the man in possession. At first United had no need of back-ups. Charlie Sagar scored a debut hat-trick as they destroyed the team expected to be their closest rivals, Bristol City, 5-1, and they won their first six league games. It seemed all the pre-season predictions of United dominating the League were to be fulfilled. But it became noticed that United were winning without dominating, by the odd goal. And then they were not winning, and gave every appearance of being 'disunited'. And then they lost, and Bristol City overtook them. Manchester United's progress was now judged 'slow and disappointing', they were suffering 'unenviable' anxiety – the 'Clayton camp is not one of the happiest'. Only Alec Bell was regularly 'magnificent', and Alec Downie was one of those open 'to much blame'. Dick was overtaken into the first team by other bright sparks, younger midfield players, but their timing was unlucky. United lost, and there was a feeling 'we cannot indulge in too many experiments'. Another defeat, and 'something will have to happen soon'. A third of the season gone, and Manchester United were trailing Bristol City, and Chelsea and West Bromwich Albion were coming up fast. United were giving their friends 'cause for anxiety': 'our old warcry has become a mockery unto us, for we are indeed very 'downhearted' … Life in the Clayton camp just now is miserable in the extreme.'

It was not just the inability of youngsters to raise their game. Established men like Downie were complacent: 'rambling is his greatest fault … And unless he alters his style a bit and takes more care of his outside man, he will find himself dropped!' Prophetic. The one advantage United had over their rivals was a large staff, so much so that it was a contemporary joke. Manchester United are like the 'old woman who lived in the shoe. They have so many players they don't know what to do.' That was indeed how the United directors' dilemma was described after another reverse: 'the directors hardly know what to do.'

They had tried most things. In thirteen league games United had included nineteen players, but not Dick Duckworth: he was not even mentioned. He was truly a forgotten man. But now his chance came. The directors decided on a 'lucky bag': five men were dropped, including Alec Downie, and Dick was in. Ten thousand watched United beat Burslem Port Vale 3-0, but Dick seemed unprepared for his big chance: 'Duckworth for Downie was a bad move.' Nevertheless, 'The Revival of the Reds' had been prompted. United went to Barnsley, and Dick had to face the talented Yorkshire left-winger George Wall. Another 3-0 win. Dick was causing jubilation in the camp. He had 'improved greatly on his previous display', and now Downie will find it 'will be a long time before ousting the local'.

Dick stayed in a 'flattering light' following a 4-0 win against newcomers Clapton Orient, and a remarkable change of fortunes continued. United's 'very effective' half-backs were pressurising Bristol City, who dropped their first point in months. On December 16th, a dismal 'fog fiend' enveloped Manchester, threatening United's first-ever match with Leeds going ahead. But the game started and the fog swept over the ground intermittently. Seventeen minutes from the end, United were leading 1-0, when Charlie Roberts was laid out by a clash of heads. When he recovered his senses he found himself alone on the field. The referee had taken everyone else off, and kept them off even when the fog again drifted away and the 14,000 crowd noisily demanded their return. It was a metaphor. Again Dick had resurrected United's prospects, and a series of vibrant wins – 3-0, 3-0, 4-0 and 3-1 – had restored their corporate confidence. But Dick disappeared with the fog: without explanation Alec Downie was back, and stayed for the big drawn games at Christmas with Chelsea and Bristol City.

Manchester United and their supporters remained nervous – the second promotion spot, lost last season, remained in doubt, as Chelsea and West Bromwich Albion were close on their heels. In these circumstances their supporters were far from patient. In fact, the Clayton crowd 'are more ready to jeer and criticise a player than to give him encouragement'. For example, when United rearranged the controversially abandoned home game with unheralded Leeds City – Dick's last appearance – it was on a quagmire. United lost, and as it was pantomime season, were inevitably called 'Humpty Dumpty'. Dick Duckworth was cast as 'all the King's men and all the King's women' when he was brought back into a ridiculed side.

The Leeds defeat was a 'positive disgrace', a 'disaster', a 'staggering blow' that opened up all the old anxieties: 'I don't know whether the

United will ever get back to the League place they have lost. No one ever dreamt [Leeds] would prove such an eye-opener for us.' Paranoia persisted: United's northern and especially Lancastrian rivals were suspected to want to avoid long trips to Chelsea and Bristol next season, and therefore would fight long and hard to keep their profitable fixtures with the big Manchester outfit, and maybe try a little less against the southerners.

This was the kind of thinking that made football a political issue, and the politicians, with a General Election imminent, agreed. There was a rash of prospective MPs kicking off matches. Many of them made a beeline for Clayton: they had the Labour candidate kicking off the first half and the Liberal Winston Churchill the second. Even Prime Minister Arthur Balfour made a 'sickly effort at setting the ball rolling' on the mud-splattered ground, and wished he had not. Not only did the crowd 'jeer at Mr Balfour's feeble effort at Clayton' but an unflattering photograph appeared in the newspapers, and Balfour lost the election. Another candidate fielded a football question, and presented a contemporary desire for temperance in all things:

'What about football fever?' shouted one of the questioners. 'With respect to that,' replied Mr Hodge, 'if you have got it, then I am sorry for you … There are many men who can talk about nothing else. I will admit that football has kept many men out of the public-houses on Saturday afternoons. It is not the game I condemn but the fever.' Nevertheless, Mr Hodge's parting shot demonstrated he knew which baby's bottom to kiss: 'And I'll tell you this, I'm coming to Denton on Saturday to kick off at your football match. I believe in everything in season.'

All this was just about tolerable, but what tipped these celebrity starts into the unacceptable was when *a lady* kicked off: 'surely we have reached the climax in these functions.'

Football fever meant many things. It meant riot and ambush. On January 27th two teams in the First League top six, Preston and Wednesday, drew 1-1 at Sheffield. A 'hostile demonstration' followed and Tom Houghton, Preston director, waited for 'the unruly spirits to get away'. Clearly not long enough:

'We had only just got outside the ground when a heavy shower of stones, cinders and mud poured down upon us from the crowd in waiting. We had barely got the length of the ground away when another large crowd, which was waiting, pelted us a second time, large heavy missiles being thrown. Lyon, the left half-back, was struck on the back of the head with a clinker, and sustained a deep scalp wound, which bled profusely. Two mounted policemen galloped alongside and escorted us on our journey. We were pelted however until we neared the centre of the city, and those missiles which struck the players and fell upon their knees were collected and handed to me [including potatoes, billiard chalks, jagged pieces of earthenware, and a pearl-hafted penknife]. We might have forgiven the threats and stone and mud throwing etc. but the occupants of every tramcar leaned over and spat in our faces as we passed. It was beastly, filthy – horrible enough to make me sick.'

In the years after the 1998 World Cup David Beckham was vilified by opposing supporters. In 1906 his predecessor as England's outside-right was Preston's Dicky Bond. And like Beckham nearly a century later, Bond could be threatened on away grounds, and with far worse violence. He had waged a running battle with Wednesday's full-back throughout the game, and came out on top with a penalty equaliser. This made him a target: 'when he was seen on the brake there were repeated cries of "Drag him off".'

Yet football fever also meant provocation and rough play. So the FA not only punished Wednesday by closing their ground but also fined each Preston player. Why? Maybe because Preston played a 'game which meant knocking the opposition off its play by sheer roughness'. Perhaps because, after the match, whilst waiting out the riot, their players 'began to make faces from the vantage point of their dressing room'.

Only a fortnight later Dick's Manchester United became the talk of the football world after a worse riot in similar circumstances. Football in the Golden Age: manly sport or mob-rule? Were its rules just? How did violence beget violence? Football's reputation was at stake.

Manchester United travelled to Bradford with a threefold agenda. First they knew City had a potent attack: they had just beaten First League Wolves 5-0 in the Cup, and largely due to flying left-winger James Conlin. Secondly, all remembered United's only previous visit to Valley Parade, when United played with 'brute force and shady tactics'. Finally, United were well aware, after another week in their training quarters, how important it was to win. The season was two thirds gone, and their much needed promotion was far from assured. Bristol City were out of sight in front, and United were only just ahead of Chelsea and West Brom. After the match their ruthless victory looked important – both their rivals lost, and United had opened up a four-point gap over the third-placed team.

Dick's teammate Bob Bonthron courted the pre-match publicity with his win-at-all-costs attitude, by making 'the frank admission that he fouled an opponent because there was no other way to prevent that opponent from scoring'. It rained heavily, and the 10,000 crowd were 'packed like herrings' under the only cover available. The ground was in a shocking condition, as was the football. 'The United did not play a sportsmanlike game' and were 'hugely lucky'. City contrived to make one 'marvellous miss' after another, and referee Tom Campbell, according to Yorkshire press and folk, was blind to the offside rule. So United led 4-1 at half-time. Chairman J J Bentley then misjudged the mood: he took a 'stroll round the ground at the interval, and on waving his umbrella to some friends, was not over well received by a certain section of the crowd'.

United felt the hostility as they came back out after the interval. The sports called out 'Play the game'; the toughs just hooted. The mood quickly worsened. First Bradford's winger got free on the last defender and advanced on goal until, just outside the penalty area, he was deliberately downed, rugby-fashion. Then immediately afterwards, 'Conlin completely outwitted both Downie and Bonthron, and was clear away for goal when Bonthron deliberately hooked the City winger's legs from under him. It was a cowardly trick, and the referee took the offender aside and cautioned him, whilst the crowd literally howled.'

This went to the heart of a problem that football had not resolved: how to punish the foul that cynically or violently prevented a goal being scored. Football's solution, the penalty kick for a foul within a defined area near the goal, was now over a decade old and already 'in such bad odour'. The rule put 'monstrous responsibility' on referees to virtually decide matches. There was so much 'inequality': officials differed on what fouls justified a penalty; they were 'set up' by the 'ridiculous claims' of players and partisans; and there had been a recent spate of penalties for more or less accidental handball: 'It is always a kind of lottery.'

But the penalty rule offered no redress here: United's defenders had deliberately offended before their opponents reached the penalty area. So the enraged crowd seethed as United scored another 'offside' goal and screamed with indignation as little Conlin met thirteen-stone Bonthron in a trial of strength which had a certain inevitable quality: 'nine stone goes to the wall, or, in this case, mother earth.'

Conlin was a star winger: within weeks the Second League player was playing in front of 102,741 at Hampden Park for England; and that summer Manchester City equalled the record transfer fee of £1,000 to sign him. Ex-Fife miner Bob Bonthron antagonised away crowds wherever he played, but this time he had gone that bit further: 'Bonthron aroused the ire of the multitude by an act of play which was certainly wrong, and Conlin was robbed of an almost sure goal.' Linesman and referee conferred, but merely spoke to Bonthron. Conlin himself had been sent off recently 'for an offence which was child's play compared to what City had endured'. It was a final straw. First, the crowd cheered lustily when City's goalkeeper fisted the ball and laid out a United forward. Then, at the end a posse of police struggled to get Bonthron and referee Campbell off the field without many would-be assailants reaching their targets. But the crowd would not be denied.

The League grounds of 1906 were dangerous places for away teams to escape from angry fans, with alcohol playing its usual part: 'every other man has a bottle of spirits in his jacket pocket ... And afterwards – well the brewers that have tied houses anywhere near a football ground know that they have a gold mine.' There were also few hiding places once the team struck out for its horse-drawn carriages to the railway station. In Bradford's narrow lanes, 'hundreds bent on mischief' congregated around the players' entrance, and posted scouts on the walls.

Bonthron, with City's secretary as escort, tried another way out, but they found themselves anticipated and cut off by an angry vengeful mob, and fled back to the dressing-tent. Then referee Campbell, with two escorts, broke cover and braved an inevitable ambush. All three were struck with ashes and mud and Campbell had 'his pipe knocked out of his mouth'. Next, Bonthron, surrounded by police, teammates, and Bradford players and officials, tried his luck: 'One man made a dash for the United back, and *aimed a direct blow at him.*' (emphasis in original)

Yet Bradford City men took the 'mobocracy's' initial brunt, first in the shape of club director John Brunt. Brunt came to the aid of Bonthron's Praetorian bodyguard, City full-back Anthony Carter, who was 'thrown to the ground in the melee ... Brunt assisted Carter to his feet and got a severe blow to the neck.' One rough got through, struck Bonthron, was immediately seized but 'with the assistance of the crowd the [assailant] tore himself loose.' City Vice-President Isaac Newton then fell ... like an apple: 'Mr Newton was then thrown to the ground and kicked several times. Meanwhile the angry hobble-de-hoys scooped up handfuls of mud and simply showered it on Bonthron, one large dose catching him full in the ear.' Charlie Roberts recalled: 'I have never experienced anything like it. I pushed several men away who were going for Bonthron. I was glad to get out of it.' Having been 'badly kicked going up the incline leading to the main street', Bonthron was rushed by the Police into the yard of the Belle Vue Hotel. The hooting, snarling crowd were left outside but enough of their stones and black slimy mud had made their mark: Bonthron was covered from head to foot in muck. They made another dash and whilst Bradford's secretary rode shotgun on Bonthron, J J Bentley and Ernest Mangnall's cab was hit by stone attacks.

Both teams afterwards took refuge in their winter training quarters at Blackpool, separated only by a narrow lane. There were no hard feelings:

indeed the twosome most often observed strolling lazily along the beach were Bob Bonthron and James Conlin. But inevitable repercussions followed. The FA convened an Emergency Commission. Everyone had something to lose. First, Bradford City had defended Bonthron heroically, but their ground faced lengthy closure. Manchester United were at risk because of 'the cool, calculating deliberation of their foul play methods', which had provoked 'the unfortunate conduct of these indiscreet youths'. And Bob Bonthron's position worsened when it became known that, like the mocking Preston players out of their dressing room window, he had spurned a chance to defuse the situation. When the crowd were baying outside, calling continually for Bonthron and Campbell to show themselves, the wisest course was to wait them out. Manchester United had a 6pm departure back to their training camp, but Bradford were taking a later train, so a safe solution was to hand: 'Bonthron was invited to stay behind and have tea with the City players and travel with them to Blackpool.'

And then it was referee versus player. On other occasions referees were suspended for failing to stamp on foul play. Otherwise they risked crowd reaction. Campbell had cautioned Bonthron but not sent him off after further assaults. Nevertheless, he identified the main source of the trouble. Bonthron followed Campbell into the inquiry, and came out having been on the wrong end of the quasi-judicial process: 'My word! That referee has been making it hot for me!'

Yet the Football Association were also under pressure. The key issue contributing to the crowd's loss of control was the lack of suitable punishment for the occasions, one fast upon the other, when City forwards were speeding hard on an unprotected goalkeeper, and were mowed down, but crucially … outside the penalty area. Its rules provided no remedy. The game was in disrepute. So with everyone in trouble, the Commission exercised discretion. Bob Bonthron was lucky, and got off. The fans were not satisfied: they still had a score to settle. When United played at Leeds months later, Bradford folk ambushed them again, this time cutting Tom Campbell's face. J J Bentley had the last, cutting word at the rugby stronghold of Yorkshire: 'Bradford spectators do not yet thoroughly understand the Association game.'

In between all this Manchester United hosted the biggest match in their short history, an English Cup-tie. Aston Villa were the giants of the modern game and United at last had an opportunity to test themselves against the best – the English Cup holders, no less. Dick Duckworth chose this auspicious communal event for a more personal celebration. Despite many weeks in Cup-tie purdah, Dick had gone a-courting, there had been a 'good response to the request for subscriptions towards a present for the occasion of his marriage and the presentation is to be made today'.

No doubt private subscriber, and club President, J H Davies, was his usual generous self, especially as he savoured a Cup-tie justifying his investment. Outside Clayton, the crowd was wild with excitement: the most 'venturesome ascended to the highest pinnacle of the telegraph pole which overlooks the ground'. When the gates were closed, forty minutes before kick off, there were '45,000 people, swaying to and fro, though I had not the slightest inclination to be One of the Swayers'. United took the lead with an own goal and, amid the great throng, the culprit, Villa's schoolmaster half-back, felt very alone: 'whilst the home patrons cheered frantically, there Pearson stood, stupefied and dismayed by the fatal result of his blunder.'

Many a defender lost their dignity at Clayton: 'he fell face forward on a particularly black patch and rose to stand a most melancholy public spectacle, wringing his hands, and dripping all over with mud.' The Cup holders, in their red and chocolate jerseys, came back, equalised and went ahead, but the referee said no, offside. It was their last chance. United surged ahead, injury reduced Villa to ten men, and United prevailed, a stunning 5-1 victory. Players were chaired off by the crowd, who hailed United's arrival among the famous clubs of English football. It was 'questionable whether Manchester United have ever won so much fame on one afternoon'.

The club had now gone further in the Cup than either they or their predecessors Newton Heath had achieved. But this prospect, and Dick's great day, graphically demonstrated the inadequacies of United's house. The crowd produced bumper receipts of £1,460 and there was another ten thousand left outside, but Clayton was ill-equipped for such grand events. It was 'nothing like up to date' and many inside saw little or nothing. The great confidence sweeping over football required tangible expression. But Clayton was not the right place and the great Cup occasion with Aston Villa began the road to the great project of its replacement – Old Trafford.

But first things first. Supreme confidence now reigned over the team's affairs. 'Nothing seems to have come amiss with United' was the theme at the beginning of March. It helped that Charlie Roberts was not picked for England's internationals. The selectors heard United's complaints that his caps had cost them promotion the previous year, and Roberts himself hit the right note: he expressed 'pleasure' at not being picked, 'as he preferred to assist his club at this critical time.' But within weeks, everything changed again. Manchester United went out of the Cup to Woolwich Arsenal, lacking 'courage and determination', and were now *third* to Chelsea in the promotion stakes. A dark cloud of depression again descended: are we once more to 'lose our chance of promotion, and see our fondest hopes crushed and unfulfilled?'

What had caused the transformation was one of those results which seemed so unlikely as to call into question either the superiority of the top footballer, or his commitment – Burslem Port Vale 1, Manchester United 0. United's followers were 'deeply indignant' at the humiliation. How could the team who beat the great Aston Villa lose to Second League stragglers? Especially after spending so long in cotton wool – 'two months special training at the seaside' – for Manchester United to 'allow itself to be beaten by an eleven of mere Staffordshire working men was surely discreditable'.

But soon United won 5-1 again and recovered second place. J H Davies, their 'presiding genius', kept his nerve and showed future confidence by writing a large cheque for Barnsley winger George Wall. Their fickle followers again became over-optimistic, all Manchester being 'painfully aware of our vacillation' as United pursued their holy grail of the First League.

The absolutely critical game came at Chelsea at Easter. United went in one point ahead, but had an extra game to play, so the Londoners needed to win. The match was enormous: some say 60,000, others 67,000 in the massive bowl of Stamford Bridge. Either way, it was the greatest crowd in the history of the Football League, and the next biggest Second League attendance that Good Friday was ten thousand.

Chelsea v Manchester United was one of two matches in the spring of 1906 which established football in London. That potential had been waiting to be tapped ever since 110,000 people went through the turnstiles at Crystal Palace to see the 1901 Cup final featuring Tottenham Hotspur. At that stage the London football scene was confused: there was one Football League club, Woolwich Arsenal, out of town in Plumstead, south-east London; several other professional outfits, like Spurs, competing in the Southern League; and various prestigious amateur clubs. The 1901 Cup final showed what was possible, and the ambitions of west London clubs Fulham and Chelsea, with their massive new grounds, built upon those possibilities.

Yet despite Chelsea's impact in their first season of existence, among the capital's potential audience there was still an air of cynicism about the northern professionals. Still a feeling that the amateur game provided the purer football. And so the northern professionals came to town mob-handed. Because why else should the Football League, representing forty clubs, choose to play their big representative match against the Scottish League in a city where, until this year, there had been just one club. London needed help, Stamford Bridge needed help, so the Football League obliged. And the players obliged with a vibrant performance which showed that tired professionals could play with the *joie de vivre* of the celebrated amateurs: English League 6, Scottish League 2. The English forwards, led by Bolton's Albert Shepherd, 'became almost instantly spokes on a wheel, and the revolutions of that wheel were a revelation. It was as if by the touch of a magician's wand powder was converted into concrete.'

'The glamour of high-class football is irresistible,' and Duckworth cemented football's capture of the capital in Manchester United's promotion decider against Chelsea on Good Friday, 1906. It was the best Easter weather for a generation. Brilliant sunshine attracted the crowds everywhere. Tramcars and river boats were packed, the city's own green spaces, parks and commons were full, railway stations were crowded and motor cars and bicycles streamed out of the capital to the nearby countryside, like Epping Forest. The only fly in the ointment was an acute dust problem. An 'endless procession of motor-cars' had overwhelmed ill-kept roads in the last few years and now, exacerbated by drought, dust 'settled in thick layers' over the main London thoroughfares like those near Stamford Bridge.

The United boys rose to the challenge and their half-backs, with Dick Duckworth at left-half, were 'excellent' against Chelsea's classy inside forwards. The game was as expected hard fought, but Jock Peddie's precise low shot put United ahead, 'to the dismay of the great crowd.' The Scot answered his critics who had been doing good business outside Clayton selling a parody of a contemporary music-hall ditty:

'Oh, stop your dribbling, Jock,
We've had enough of you,
You're always dribbling, dribbling, dribbling, dribbling,
Stop your dribbling do.'

Chelsea equalised, but it was not enough. United were promoted, after eleven years in the Second League. It was a portentous moment: within days Vesuvius erupted, destroying villages and threatening Naples; and an earthquake razed San Francisco to the ground.

Manchester United's final fixture was a cause of rejoicing. Bills advertising the game carried an added message: 'Welcome the new First League team.' Clayton's grandstand was bedecked with spring flowers, and United took the field to a rendition of 'See the Conquering Hero Comes'. Dick Duckworth did 'rare good work. From him, new left-winger George Wall received a nice pass, and sailing past Wood in grand style banged the ball past Starbuck at great speed. Loud and long were the cheers.' Six times the process was repeated: a 'glorious victory,' and then a celebratory invasion – 'the players made an effort to escape what they knew was coming, but they were intercepted and borne with wild fantastic triumph to the dressing-rooms. The way was speedily blocked, and some of the men were tossed about for several minutes, the most unhappy victors that one could imagine. Moger, the giant goalkeeper, alone escaped the ordeal. No sooner was the whistle blown for the last time than he leapt over the barrier and fled, apparently, out of the ground altogether.'

Later, appearing from 'the office over the stand, all the men received special cheers for their magnificent work', and later still a souvenir medal. 'Fireworks, balloons, rattles, red and white tall hats, umbrellas and favours, decorations, a new First League flag,' and, amid all the cheering, speeches, from J H Davies and J J Bentley, on the prospects for next year. Because of course, in football, the next year is always a new start.

Chapter Three

# Jack Jones's Locker: Professional Football in The Golden Age

October 1903. The month in which Dick Duckworth became a professional was one in which one colliery sacked 78 miners. On September 1st, the traditional start of the football season, they had absented themselves from work to watch their local First League match. It was a risky thing to do. Unemployment was increasing daily, the beginnings of a slump that would bite hard on working people during 1904 and 1905. In particular, the weaving mills of Lancashire, where Dick plied his trade, were losing money. Conditions in the cotton trade, Manchester's emblematic industry, were 'worse than during the cotton panic of forty years ago', when the American Civil War threatened its very existence. The magistrates who considered the miners' case pondered their foolishness: 'they had heard so much about there being no work, yet here was excellent work and the men would not have it.' That same day their employers reduced miners' wages by ten per cent.

Football in the Golden Age was inescapably industrial. Dick played on a ground literally covered with smoke, steam and grime; and travelled from game to game in trains reeking of the same tastes and smells. The clubs had but recently emerged out of teams of heavy industrial workers, like the railwaymen of Newton Heath/Manchester United. Their core support was a rough-tongued, disabused working class. In retrospect it was a betrayed class. England's industry was already in decline, the capital generated at home being invested abroad. And in October 1903, the economic relationship between home and abroad, between Britain and its colonies, was an issue of major debate. The day's foremost politician, Joseph Chamberlain, hijacked the political agenda with a series of high-profile speeches up and down the country, initiating 'fiscal fever'. If Dick's first Football League match was watched by only a thousand people, nine thousand would cram into halls to listen to Chamberlain. His theme was Tariff Reform, preserving the Empire by establishing the basis of preferential trade with the colonies. Protectionism or Free Trade? It dominated the terms of British economic politics until the Depression of the 1920s.

Dick Duckworth's football career mirrored this battle between Free Trade and Protectionism. On the one hand, there were those who advocated Free Trade, the untrammelled action of the capitalist marketplace. Overtly this was the language of top footballers, like Dick's star teammate Billy Meredith, who argued a player should be paid whatever an employer thought he was worth, without restriction of a wider authority. However, the protectionists sought to contain the financial advantages of the likes of Manchester United. Such clubs were often depicted as robber barons, overwhelming competitors, exploiting their workers, contaminating the very nature of their business – 'protected against all and sundry by the sheer weight of the money which the people they robbed of their players would help them to earn.'

And the business of football clubs was sport. What was sport in this context? Who represented sport, who looked after it? Sport, football, was like the ideals of Empire, and the Football Association protected those ideals. The Football League by contrast was a cartel, struggling to contain its contradictions: between the desire of the big clubs for freedom from financial restriction, and that of the smaller clubs for a protected equality that would maintain individual financial viability and the integrity of the whole League.

Dick Duckworth also lived his career through a social landscape of clamorous protest. October 1903 was the same month, in the same city, in which Emmeline Pankhurst formed the Women's Social and Political Union – the Suffragettes. Their decade of disruption and sabotage grew to a crescendo in the last active year of Dick's career. 1903 also saw the first victory by the Labour Party in a three-cornered parliamentary fight with Liberals and Conservatives. The winner was a former moulder, just like Dick Duckworth. The growth of the Labour and Trade Union movements gained momentum from a scandal in 1904 and 1905.

The imperialist British Government had connived with mine owners to import 100,000 Chinese labourers to South Africa and imprison them in compounds ruled by fear and punishment, only freed to work in the mines. Nothing could be more calculated to inflame the toiling millions at home, who were increasingly challenging the view of labour as mere commodity. The power of this image was still felt in 1912, when a commentator imagined how professional footballers would be treated in the year 2000. He saw men imprisoned in compounds ruled by fear and punishment, only freed from their shackles in order to play in front of vast crowds.

A new electorate saw the insults behind such scandals and perceived a Conservative Party split asunder by the war between protectionist

Joseph Chamberlain and Free Trader Lord Rosebery. The result was an unprecedented landslide defeat for the Conservatives in the General Election of 1906, and an inadequate recovery in 1910. The bitter loss saw the Conservatives retreat to their innate majority in the House of Lords, where they began a guerrilla parliamentary campaign that betrayed a lack of scruple for fair play among the highest in the land. Their parliamentary bill-wrecking in turn destroyed confidence within the labour movement that constitutional action could meet their needs. Thus the end of the Edwardian decade saw an explosion of 'direct action', 'lightning strikes' and industrial sabotage by trade union activists.

And all through this period the Irish Problem became more and more intractable, and on the Continent the conflicts and tensions led inexorably to a European and World War. It was an age imbued with the spirit of revolt. The years from 1906-14 witnessed a crescendo of rule-breaking: by labour strikers; by the House of Lords; by the Ulster and Irish volunteers; and by the Suffragettes.

Football too was of this age. Football was passionate about rules and rule-breaking. Its history was of making rules, especially those that distinguished it from rugby. But there were written rules, and then the interpretations of rules, the meanings behind rules, the spirit behind rules. Football in the Golden Age was an unceasing tumult. The rules were at stake in each and every match. One example. In 1905 referee Harrower created a stir by showing the 'judgement of Solomon'. He sent off an assailant not at the point of the foul itself but when his injured victim had to leave the field, and his opponents went down to ten men. His detractors said he was wrong, and the incident served to reinforce the alternative idea of the thing itself; that the foul either did, or did not, deserve a sending off. The effect on the victim, or his team, was a matter of chance, and should not enter into the referee's consideration.

On the other hand, football's institutions wanted to emphasise official Edwardian virtues: maturity, stability, respectability. J J Bentley, President of the Football League, Vice-Chairman of the Football Association, Chairman of Manchester United, saw only continuity when, in 1905, he surveyed organised football's first thirty years. Whereas a county cricketer would find his sport unrecognisable, football was 'the only game that has changed so little'. The positions on the field, goalkeeper, two backs, three half-backs, five forwards, were the same as in 1880: it is 'considered almost a crime to alter the position of your forces, if even temporarily'.

J J Bentley had been an indispensable go-between for football's power blocs, League and Football Association. He first encountered a small clique of 'gentlemen' running the FA, opposed to anything 'provincial'.

Bentley was the means by which the 'provincials' who ran the League asserted themselves, so that he could be complacent in 1905: the two organisations had been through periods of 'jealousy and rivalry' to reach a 'reasonable', 'common-sense' accommodation (Bentley, J J 1905, in Leatherdale, 1997, pp.11-14). The Football Association was the original authority and remained final arbiter on the rules. The FA in 1903-13 still bore the hallmarks of its origins among the public schools and universities, and its most notable figures, President Lord Kinnaird and Chairman Charles Clegg, were both players in the internationals and Cup finals of the 1870s. The FA's relationship with professional football was always problematic. By 1909 Manchester United's Charles Roberts could write that in six years in the game he had never heard one player say a good thing about the Football Association.

Professional football first challenged the Football Association in 1885, when it was forced to confront what had been an open secret for years: that some clubs paid their players. The FA only accepted professionalism when it became apparent that their control over football was threatened, and then watched uneasily as the clubs set up a Football League in 1888 that provided the basis for a viable professionalism. Leagues were a conceptual triumph and a marketing success, but even so attendances were rarely out of single figure thousands. Financial survival was not assured.

The Football League was based on a season of fixtures between teams who were relatively evenly matched. Soon a tension grew between the principle of fair sporting competition and the advantages given by wealth and depth of population support to some clubs to secure better players. In the end this came down to payment *for* players, in transfer fees, and *to* players, in wages. By the turn of the century these tensions, and their expression through players' wages, were seen to threaten the competitive equality and financial viability of football: 'it would ultimately mean the collapse of the League.' The answer was a maximum wage (Dobbs, B 1973, p.56). The majority of small and medium-sized clubs in the Football League decided to limit the players' weekly wage; and the Football Association, always eager to assert even competition and sporting tradition over overt commercial advantages, supported them.

The imposition of the maximum wage was also a riposte to the perceived growing power of the professional footballer as a working man. The relationship between the paid footballer and his sport was the heart of many controversies and debates in the Golden Age: in committee and boardrooms; in newspaper offices; in pubs and the grounds themselves. Why does the professional footballer play? For an amateur, nominally the question was straightforward – for the love of the game, for the exercise of skills; for the thrill of competition. But a professional? For the money, an easy life, what? And how can a watcher know if he is trying his best?

From a pure sporting sense, the maximum wage put all players and all clubs on the same footing. And it worked. The style of football more and more emphasised team play. Play became harder and faster. League championships featured even contests and close finishes, and the Cup competitions regularly featured small clubs defeating big ones. And clubs benefited financially: in the three years before the maximum wage, medium-sized Wolverhampton Wanderers lost almost £400; in the three years afterwards they made almost £500.

As the big clubs failed to reverse the rule, they sank their profits into a new generation of designer grounds. It was all they could do: 'Everton has so much money that she does not know what to do with it. She is not allowed to pay higher wages or give bigger dividends.' So in the summer of 1906, as Dick and Manchester United waited to take their First League place, there were major ground improvements everywhere – St Andrews in Birmingham, at both Liverpool clubs, and an impressive new double-decker stand at Blackburn. Clayton made only minor changes.

Within the community of football players, there was some ambivalence. At one level throughout the decade of Dick's career professional players were unanimously against the maximum wage. Their level and structure of payment became increasingly anachronistic as attendances grew, club profits increased, and impressive new stadia sprouted up.

But within a team it was not so straightforward. The maximum wage regime led to better team spirit. Previously the rank and file pros were often 'sullenly indifferent' towards the better-paid stars: 'the men with the wages did least and expected the men with less wages to do the donkey work … Spoiling the effectiveness of the teams … by introducing, just beneath the surface, the spirit of jealousy and envy – just that sense of wrong which rankled, perhaps unconsciously, and killed the feeling of oneness which is the foundation of perhaps the most democratic game of the day.'

On the other hand there was an awareness that the increasing speed of professional football, and the consequent physical clashes, made it a precarious business. One article pointed out how few players from the 1899-1900 season were still around in Dick's first season, 1903-04, and the rarity of players completing a decade in top football was acknowledged: ''Tis the pace that kills.' Likewise the frequency of career-ending injuries might be accepted with equanimity by commentators as 'the fortune of war', but the players themselves, and their families, naturally aimed to limit the risk.

What did these developments say about the motivation of the professional player? It was not just a matter of the level of weekly wages: Edwardian moralists were equally against bonuses – they saw it as being paid twice for the same work. So pros had no monetary incentive to win, either a match or a competition, or even play in any given match. Professionals, even ones friendly to the authorities, wrote in the newspapers that without a monetary incentive to play well, a player had every reason not to take too many risks, to say he was injured or even prefer to play in the reserves. He got the same whatever he did and, just as important as leagues got bigger, they got paid the same even when they played more than one game a week. But if teammates started to feel some players were not trying as hard as they ...

There was widespread doubt that reality matched appearances. Clubs, after all, were still under the same competitive pressures and the players were the means of that competition. If somehow, by breaking the rules clubs could get or keep better players, or get them to try or play harder, they were tempted – especially if they thought their competitors were doing so. If it helped that your players felt looked after, then ... Some of this was debated officially. What, for example, counted as a bonus? Gold medals were accepted as recognising sporting achievement, but not other presents 'in kind', like pianos or jewellery. So clubs widened their horizons. When Liverpool took their players on a pre-season Continental tour it was widely accepted as a holiday thank you for the 1906 championship success.

There was one officially sanctioned payment that became increasingly important, and potentially lucrative, and that was the benefit. If the pro had completed five years service *and* at the discretion of club and FA, he could keep the receipts of a selected match. In October 1903 Charlie Sagar and Joe Leeming each took a benefit. They were top players. Sagar played for England, and Leeming did not miss a match for five seasons. Between them they scored three of the six unanswered goals by which Bury had won the Cup that spring and both played in Bury's 1900 4-0 Cup final victory. Sagar and Leeming each received a £109 benefit, and immediately had to treat everyone to dinner – directors, officials, players, even the reserves. By the end of the decade benefits realised £250, £500, even £800, yet the maximum wage remained £4 a week. This bounty awaited Dick Duckworth – but only if he could stay with Manchester United until October 1908.

The maximum wage era aroused endemic suspicion. Was it reasonable to believe that star players previously paid £5, £6 or £7 would simply reconcile themselves to being paid just £4? Or that players would seek or consent to transfers involving them moving hundreds of miles for the official £10 signing on fee? The Edwardian decade was littered with FA inquiries that confirmed the widespread rule-breaking of financial regulations that everyone suspected. Sometimes this rule-breaking attracted draconian punishment, sometimes not. Generally, admitting your guilt made the difference.

Others felt the corruption was revealed by the players' collective passivity. Year after year the big clubs tried to remove the limits on bonuses, signing-on and re-signing fees, and year after year they failed. Commentators observed the social scene, saw how other workers were organising to remedy their grievances, and wondered 'if players are keen to end the wage limit, why don't they strike? In blunt English, the pros don't seem to have pluck enough.'

But there is a danger in establishing a sense that football's reality did not match appearances. The millions who attended matches every year needed to believe, and believe each and every match. For the players not to try was the worst crime, especially if it could be laid at the door of illegal payment requests: 'I accepted the result with incredulity and – said things. I have learned since that before the team went on the field they asked for a bonus if they won. Their request was very promptly and very rightly refused, and the team – lost!'

Similarly two sides met in a Lancashire Cup-tie only two days after bruising First League matches. One put out their best side, the other did not. People of course paid to watch and judge them: 'the question kept rising to one's lips, 'Are the men trying?' … Nothing short of disgraceful … Such a burlesque that merited all the uncomplimentary remarks it provoked.' The ignominy was directed at the winners because it took them too long to defeat inferior opponents. Why did games not follow an expected course? Was there something more to it? And sometimes there was. Dick's most notable colleague, Billy Meredith, attempted to bribe opponents so that his then team Manchester City could win the 1905 championship.

References to bribery within the game were not uncommon. The famous footballing cricketer, C B Fry, in the course of a tirade against the game's association with drink and gambling, accused a goalkeeper of being bribed to throw a Cup-tie. Club officials accused their own players but, fearing legal reprisals, promptly withdrew, saying they had merely repeated gossip. Even a ringing endorsement of football's essential integrity – 'the public get a straight run for their money' – carried the sting in its tail that twelve games had been rigged since football became popular.

The decade of Dick's career also saw an explosion of gambling on football matches, all of it illegal, and therefore all the more difficult to know its boundaries. The origins of football pools were laid in these years, but there was informal betting on each match. Understandably it made crowds even more engaged, and even more dependent on players trying their best.

If the professional footballer inhabited an ambivalent position, what did it say about football? The Edwardian era still experienced a tension about sport. Did its values essentially apply to the participant, or could they be shared with the watcher? A player learnt respect: for the rules, the authorities that enforced the rules, his teammates, his opponents, and the luck which brought either defeat or victory. The watcher however increasingly valued entertainment, thrills and expertise. Time and again football moralists said they preferred football to be amateur, but not at the cost of an inferior standard of play. Social moralists like Baden-Powell, founder of the scout movement, asserted the greater virtues of playing over watching: 'too many spectators, too few players.'

Players were often depicted as much victims as exploiters of the game's popularity. Professional football was only a momentary phase in a man's life when they were mere 'fighting cocks': 'Mr Spectator, is it morally right that, just for your sport and pleasure on a Saturday afternoon, these young fellows should be seduced from their favourable and daily toil.' There was nonetheless gratitude that young men or boys identified so keenly with sport: 'very few youths indeed give recreation the cold shoulder altogether – the fewer the better for the British Empire.' Watching was defended as a lesser evil: a Saturday afternoon football match stopped the working man spending his time and money on drink, and thus prevented domestic violence or penury.

The moralists often expressed the latent fear of the mob in relation to football crowds. A dominating theme of the later Victorian age was the fear that the underclass would overwhelm the propertied and respectable classes. Many changes in political and social life were intended to head off this threat. Football was not intentionally political, but the passions it engendered might have unintended consequences. Football engaged the commitment of the working class to a worrying extent. In a moment 'vulpine and sodden fans' would move from 'savage joy' through 'malignant anxiety' to 'frantic disappointment'. It seemed impossible to square these behaviours with Olympian ideals of sport. Crowds exhibited 'ungenerous one-sided enthusiasm': full of 'spiteful yells', 'torrents of foul abuse' and an easy disposition towards a 'fierce brandishment of sticks and fists'.

The nature of football as it had emerged – each player with his own position, his own tasks, his distinctive contribution to the whole – has been seen to mirror the increasingly compartmentalised nature of contemporary industrial work. But contemporaries also saw the links between work and leisure behaviour of the watchers, and saw in its passion something foreign and un-English. By the spring of 1905 football was unequivocally *the* sport of English society. A prominent populist politician and sometime Government Minister, 'Honest John' Burns, went to the Crystal Palace to watch the 1905 Cup final, a match won by an all-English eleven for the first time since 1893:

'One's mind instinctively reverted to the clangour as the voices rose and fell to Greece, Rome and Spain, and one thought of the amphitheatre – the circus, the arena, the bull-ring, the prize-ring; and now its tamed, subdued and potentially dangerous successor, the vast gathering of City workers, who through being over-specialised in their work, have become over-athleticised in their play. This is a serious portent, and brings the working class in their games nearer to that point which Matthew Arnold feared when he had apprehensions of 'an upper-class materialised, a middle-class vulgarised, and a working-class brutalised'.

Could the middle class civilise football? These hopes centred on London. Professional football had been seen as an essentially northern phenomenon but 1905 saw plans for two massive stadia in the imperial capital, London. First Fulham, then 'a vast auditorium at Stamford Bridge, with a holding capacity of 150,000 persons. The best that the provinces can do pales by comparison ... The Association code is thriving and prosperous everywhere. Its popularity is unbounded.'

The interplay between, on the one hand, respectable notions and appearances, and on the other, commercial imperatives and the threat of wilder emotions, was demonstrated during a Spurs Cup run in the Golden Age. Until Chelsea's emergence, Tottenham Hotspur had carried London's standard from the Southern League. Football's full potential was revealed when an extraordinary crowd of over 110,000 people attended Spurs' 1901 Cup final at Crystal Palace. London was no longer immune, and nor were the 'better taste'. 'Lord Stanley and a fashionable party gave further *eclat*' to an Everton v Spurs Cup clash in 1904. Spurs prevailed and in the next round hosted another Football League giant, Aston Villa. Spurs 'bungled' the arrangements and a 'rowdy crowd' of 40,000 broke in. The match was secretly declared a friendly but the players were required to play as if it were still a Cup-tie. They failed to convince. The crowd were not fooled and forced an abandonment. Spurs were doubly punished: being fined the very considerable sum of £350 for admitting so many people who had no chance of seeing play – 'equivalent to taking [money] for something which was not on sale' – and having to replay in Birmingham.

The Spurs hero of that replay – literally playing the game of his life – also illustrated another aspect of the precariousness of an Edwardian footballer. Jacky Jones's winner was the goal of the season, and his last ever. Seconds from the end 'the Hotspur right made a dash, and the ball was ballooned up in the direction of Jones. He was on it like a cat, and Alec Leake lunged at him and tripped him. The referee whipped his whistle to his mouth, but Jones had kept his balance, and next moment, Miles, the Villa back, tore himself at the little forward, who drew his left foot back just in time to evade the contact. Quick as the eyes could follow the action, Jones had drawn the ball with his left foot to his right toe – then a sharp, high shot, and the game was won. Jones was almost torn to pieces by his colleagues, who kissed him and hugged him in their joy. Trembling with pent-up emotion, great tears were rolling down the forward's cheeks when he toed the centre line again and once inside the tent he broke down and wept like a child.'

Jacky Jones did not make the kick off for the next season – he had died of typhoid fever. Soon afterwards another professional, Nicol Smith, of Glasgow Rangers and Scotland, died suddenly: 'of fine proportion physically, he was just the man to catch the eye ... Now his earthly career has been cut short by a fatal attack of enteric fever ... It shows that a man who is apparently in the best possible health may be cut off at short notice. The moral is plain to everybody.' Ironically, Nicol played for Scotland in the England international of 1902 in which 26 spectators were killed and 500 injured, an event directly attributed to football's attraction – 'the thrill of excitement, the general craning of necks, and the wild rush to get a glimpse of the flying Templeton, that produced the strain on the timbers which led to the terrible Ibrox disaster.'

Another glimpse of the headway football was making with the higher echelons of society occurred in and around the Alps one mid-Edwardian spring. In a fashionable hotel in Milan on a Monday evening a group of English tourists gathered in formal dress for dinner, and were startled at the conversational gambit of one of the gentlemen: 'I wonder who's won the Cup?' The next day, on the other side of the Gothard Pass, another 'gentleman' read an English translation paper containing an account of Saturday's final. Seated in the corner of the cable car as it neared the summit, he observed with English *sang froid*, 'Everton won the Cup.'

But on a material level professional football was about the relationship of players and clubs, complicated by the existence of a third force, representing the established soul of the game, the Football Association. The FA especially hated and wanted to constrain the transfer system. At the level of sport this seemed akin to teams buying success, and at an individual level the sportsman had become commodity, the free Englishman somewhat less so.

For individual footballers the effect could be devastating. Sam McAlister ended up in a police cell when no one would pay the fee his club demanded. Burnley offered him fifty shillings a week but only £5 for his transfer when Grimsby wanted £30. McAlister was 'in dire straits': not a half-penny in his pocket, his wife about to have a baby, his landlady threatening to put them out on the streets.

McAlister was pursuing the off-chance of a game with Accrington Stanley when temptation, or necessity, struck: 'for the miserable difference of £25 he was kept idle and … to keep himself from starvation stole a pair of boots. To think that football clubs should be able to put a price on the head of a player and thus keep him in their thrall is a shameful travesty of sport … never contemplated by those who laboured for the legislation of professionalism over twenty years ago. The system is not only un-English, but it opens the door to much fraud and deceit covertly practised.' The system contravened British concepts of individual freedom and fair play, and carried an image of the working man *vis à vis* his employer which the rising labour movement was struggling to eradicate.

Each summer saw unsuccessful attempts by the big clubs to end the limits on pay. Aston Villa led the way, often on the basis of their inability to reward their players properly. For example, in 1906, they complained their players had produced £10,000 profits in the last two seasons, of 'which they could under the existing rules have no share'. Not only that, these players were only precariously protected by the club. Aston Villa had experienced a decade of triumphs – four championships and three Cup wins – but had disappointed in 1906 – not least in going out of the Cup at Second League Manchester United. So when at their AGM the Villa announced 'all the best players have been retained', the response was 'roars of manic laughter' from the shareholders, who shouted back 'old crocks, you mean'.

Individuals were often in contradictory positions. Manchester United's nominal leader was its chairman, J J Bentley. Like many contemporaries he rode many horses – Chairman of a club, President of the Football League, member of the FA Council, former referee and club secretary, publisher and editor of entrepreneurial sporting newspapers. As Aston Villa proposed the end of the maximum wage rule for the umpteenth time, J J Bentley said he supported them from United's point of view, but not from the League's.

The basic restriction upon a professional footballer was that the club which held his registration was the only club for which he could play. There were two authorities involved: his club's league (the Southern or Football League), and the Football Association. The club registration had to be reaffirmed each May in a specific contract for the following season. Once a player signed on again no other club could approach him; but there was that moment, at the end of each season, when he was approachable. If the player was persuaded to move, and the other club was in the Football League, then a fee was payable for the transfer of his registration. But if the club was in another league then he might be obtained without a fee. But could the player be persuaded? That introduced further complications. First, when he initially signed his club paid him a £10 fee, but that was all: officially there was no further fee for signing again for the next season, although that commonly occurred. Secondly, why should a player already on the maximum wage move to another club, without a share in the transfer fee? No reason.

Yet the reality was that by 1906 football's increased wealth was being invested in an inflated transfer market. Clubs were willing to pay £500 'on the off chance of getting a real gem, even in the rough', and there was an army of agents roaming the land with commissions to sign players. Agents who would 'wax fat on money which "cannot be paid": 'I was only the other day offered a job which could have involved £600 for only a moderate half-back, whilst I knew of a case in which I could transfer a certain back straight off the reel for £850, and make a nice little sum for myself.' The end of the season was the time at which clubs decided upon the players for the next: tried to hold on to existing men, and attract new ones. Those not offered a new contract were 'down on their luck'. Unless they got another club they were finished.

Wanted players were in a strong but unstable bargaining position. There were two employers' cartels, the Football League and the Southern League, and every year, each were 'on the prowl', aiming to poach men without paying a transfer fee. Players naturally played off one against the other. Directors complained that men asked for the maximum wage of £4 a week and an illegal £100 for signing on: '[such and such a club] are ready to give me £50, and I can get £75 from [another club]. I'd rather go to you for £100.' There's roguery somewhere. Agents are about.'

The only recourse of a club who lost such a player was to retain him on its list of registered players, and wait. Wait until the player came north again, when his original club could seek a share of the transfer fee. The volume of activity was high. In 1906 First Division clubs retained 800 players: the smallest staff was Bristol City's – seventeen – and the largest Aston Villa's *ninety*. Manchester United had the most players in the category of retained but not actively offered a contract (i.e. they were playing down south) – an extraordinary 57 (as against forty players retained more conventionally).

In these circumstances it was understandable that no one stuck to the 'existing rules'. There were two types of avoidance: one outside the spirit, but technically within the rules, the other flagrant abuse. Middlesbrough illustrates both. In both 1904 and 1905, just as in previous seasons, they seemed certain to be relegated from the First League, which would cost them £4,000. To avoid this in 1904 they paid the first thousand-pound transfer fee for Alf Common, and miraculously stayed up. The action was 'almost unanimously condemned in the Press'. The transfer and its motivation were 'barefaced artifice'. In 1905 they did the same thing: right at the end of the season, and despite being £2,000 in debt, they bought their way out of trouble, signing three star forwards, including England's most famous professional, Steve Bloomer. Again Boro's action had contravened both the nature of sport – 'seeking to upset fair competition' – and the brotherly altruistic nature of the Football League – a 'flagrant violation of the self-denying compact'.

No one believed that Alf Common and Steve Bloomer joined Middlesbrough's desperate relegation battles for a £10 signing fee. Unsurprisingly, Boro were one of many clubs fined for paying illegal bonuses in a decade of many FA inquiries.

Several inquiries were made into Manchester United, but not just because of illegal payments. The Football Association was suspicious of the risen United because it was a 'one-man concern'. J H Davies was unusual in club football in being so obviously the man with the power and the money, yet he had to hide it. Affiliation to the Football Association was for sporting clubs, with appropriate constitution and practices. Davies came into football with no previous interest at a time when a new combination of more controllable costs and increasing popularity promised profits to reward investment. He was told the club would cost him a thousand pounds a year, but it turned out to be far more. United did not break even until, in 1906-07, it reached the First League, and three years later seasonal receipts had doubled to £18,000. The Football Association would not accept an individual running a club, or a club being run for speculative commercial reasons. Changes were required to constitution and accounts. Manchester United's means of acceptability was J J Bentley. His chairmanship symbolically linked the club to the mainstream of both the Football League and Football Association, and he 'personally guaranteed' the rightness of their accounts.

So it was not Manchester United which was decimated by the Football Association as the 1906-07 season approached – it was Manchester City (Green, G 1978, p.218). Both suffered FA inquiries into possible financial irregularities, and fared very differently. United's 'fixer' Harry Stafford fell on his sword, and, alone, was suspended for two and a half years, admitting paying wages 'in advance'. This meant players had received illegal payments (probably including Dick Duckworth), so some wondered why none were suspended. All agreed United had got off lightly, and that J J Bentley had 'kept his hands clean'. City however were torn apart, kicking and screaming in denial. Seventeen players were fined up to £100: a century later players of City's status might earn £40,000, not £4, a week which would make the fine equivalent to a million pounds. They were also suspended from football until January 1907, and then would have to be sold to other clubs.

So just as Dick Duckworth's Holy Grail was reached, Manchester itself was revealed as a 'cesspool ... the home of the hydra-headed monster of corruption'.

Town Directorate: "Now, have I an offer for this one?"

The Football Association have broken into the privacy of Middlesbrough.

£ s d. [Top] What am I bid ...? When Grimsby sold their star player Charlie Roberts to United the imagery of a slave auction was irresistible.
[Bottom] Middlesbrough were caught out in the FA's ongoing fight with clubs over the reality and appearance of football finances. United's turn would come

Tom Webster was a top sports cartoonist for half a century. [Left] When Dick's 'new' Manchester United (represented by the Cottonopolis symbol) strung up Villa on New Year's Day 1907, he saw a warning of what was to come. [Right] When Dick's English League won 6-1 in 1910, the beat-up Irish looked to Nationalist politicians to even scores. The caption reads 'Be jabers, but it's about toime Mishter Redmond saw to this'

United stalwarts struggled in the First League.
[Left, top and bottom] Bob Bonthron found toughness was not enough. [Right, top and bottom] Alec Downie scored against Arsenal but was often left on his backside

Manchester derby moments. [Top] Dick is too late as Irvine Thornley (England international/Players' Union delegate) scores for Manchester City against United. [Bottom] Billy Meredith and Jim Blair square up

Footballers as Supermen, 1956.
Sport was a double-edged sword. Edwardians feared that, fifty years on, 'the mass of people are puny and effeminate, and the only strong ones are those paid to perform athletic feats'

The Eight Ages of the Edwardian Footballer. '1: The Boy – what may he become? Ask the Team Manager behind the tree. 2: After a season or two he leaves for a famous club. 3: His first appearance is a huge success, but – 4: His quickly secured new friends spoil his training. 5: He receives an apologetic caution from the Chairman. 6: He reaches the zenith of his career and becomes an international. 7: His benefit follows. 8: Finally he accepts a position as a trainer'

CHAPTER FOUR

# 1906-07
# INTO THE VORTEX: A PROMISE FULFILLED

The new Manchester City literally melted away at the beginning of the 1906-07 season. September 1st was extraordinarily hot. Survivors like Irvine Thornley and new signings like James Conlin all found the 'intense heat' too much, and were overcome. After half-time only six men came out of the dressing-tent: 'Conlin at length appeared with his white cloth headgear.' City's new Scottish recruits were no more resilient: 'another very clever bit of bric-a-brac to ornament our costly sideboard.' One of these, 'disinclined to play after the interval,' was eventually persuaded to return but 'succumbed at last and required a cold douche with the sponge to get him to his feet … He risked sunstroke and a possible illness by remaining.' Two days later they lost 1-9 – thirteen goals conceded in the first two matches of a new era! Three years later, having spent £7,000 on a new side, City were relegated, and they still blamed the Football Association.

United would have to assume the mantle of Manchester's First League pride. They started respectably, but expectation was high and only eight goals in six matches was not enough: 'Wanted: Goal Scorers … When it comes to scoring goals the men could not do it.'

Dick Duckworth had not featured in the first team but now he emerged, unexpectedly, to answer United's fervent prayer: Stoke City 1, Dick Duckworth 2. His chance came when United were struck hard by an epidemic of colds: Dick was their eighteenth player in only seven matches. His goals were opportunist, one followed an 'exciting scrimmage' and the other a 'finishing touch' after the goalkeeper saved the original shot. While 'Duckworth did not play a great game at Stoke in the novel position of outside right he performed the two things needed – got the goals for his side'. Dick was at half-back as the bottom club forced a 1-1 draw at Clayton. Some thought it was unfair for Dick to be moved around but 'no matter where he is he is always a trier': 'I am a great admirer of Duckworth, but he is not possessed of all the virtues and attributes necessary to qualify him to occupy every position with complete success … He is a splendid fellow and a good trier, but is not getting the chance.'

For the next game Dick was a forward again and United lost 1-4: 'in all conscience we have tried changes and experiments enough.'

Elsewhere, at Elland Road, David Wilson, a Boer War veteran, headed the ball, was injured and left the field. He returned then retired once more and died in the dressing room. Mrs Wilson had been watching the game. There was dispute about the cause of death: the coroner found 'heart failure due to over-exertion at football'. Someone who knew Wilson's style of twisting himself to get more force into heading the ball, argued he died from 'rupture of the spinal cord'.

Dick suffered from United's supporters being 'sick and tired' of the lack of progress. He was left out for a loss at Everton; showed 'to great advantage' beating Woolwich Arsenal; but was less effective in a 2-5 defeat to Sheffield Wednesday. United now abandoned shuffling their pack and signed Alex Menzies from Hearts, Scotland's current centre-forward, to replace Dick. Dick's prospects looked increasingly ominous: 'not that I would deprecate the exhibition given by our general utility man, Duckworth.' But United continued to have a 'rough time of it just now', with all the regulars under scrutiny. For example, Bob Bonthron and Alec Downie 'got in each other's way': 'Downie rambles a lot, and leaves his outside man unmasked ... So to it, Alex.'

Dick came back for the biggest game of the season. It was Manchester's great day: the first derby in the First League, the first game between City and United in their modern identities. Every avenue to Hyde Road was choke-full, every hansom cab was overloaded: 'if it is true that the ground will accommodate fifty thousand, 50,000 were there without a doubt.' An hour before the start, the ground was packed and 'still they come'. The gates were closed: the gate was £1,100 – 'a solid human mass stretched from the airy top of the terracing to the deep, distant touchline ... another mighty crowd of many thousand people surged and shouted and argued impotently outside ... one of the gates was broken down, but the rush was not a bad one.'

These early derbies were difficult to report. One journo, whose initial view was 'obscured ... by one of the thick posts which support the stand', had 'a bone to pick with the United club'. Eventually placed in a 'dirty pen', he 'objected to having to work amongst a lot of partisans, and particularly with ladies standing on the seat in front', not to mention their large hats (Cawley and James, 1991). In similar fashion, many United fans were confined to the 'dreary spaces under the viaduct' to watch their team's expected 'drubbing'.

Another journalist was comfortable enough to reflect upon the decisive episode. Dick Duckworth was a protagonist in the key duel, between

United's backs and City's wingers. Dick's latest role carried Shakespearean responsibilities: 'never before had he had such importance thrust upon him.' Some thought the expectations were 'unfair': 'I quite admire Duckworth as a good reserve half, with a decided leaning to the right, but a left-back he certainly is not.' Some thought Dick 'rose to the occasion ... but Bonthron, in his efforts to help him, weakened his own position'. Dick's main opponent was George Stewart, Scotland's current right-winger. Bob Bonthron faced his old nemesis, James Conlin, 'as tricky as a monkey.' Conlin first tested Dick, and was 'cleverly stopped', so switched back to giving Bonthron a 'rare gruelling'. The big impetuous Scot was running headlong into the role of scapegoat.

As against Conlin for Bradford City only months before, Bonthron 'lost his head at the merciless gibing with which the crowd rewarded his efforts to stop his old enemy'. Left 'blundering behind' once more, Bob miskicked wildly into his own goal – a 'glaring blunder'. Bonthron 'made a savage gesture with his fists at one of his colleagues who ventured to reproach him ... [and said] something that could not be nice to the unfortunate' goalkeeper Harry Moger.

Journalists sitting comfortably could be inspired into reverie: 'Bonthron both punched and kicked the ball and said things. It reminds me of a colleague who was playing golf the other day, and who was pulling the drives, finding all the bunkers, pulling his approach shots and missing the easiest of putts. Eventually he could stand it no longer, and he took his ball to a quiet part of the course, and there hammered it into the ground with an iron, while he apostrophised it in language which was not exactly parliamentary. I think that is what Bonthron would have liked to do with that football! ... he could do nothing right afterwards ... but he did not spare himself and ran himself absolutely to a standstill.'

Matters did not improve: 'when he returned to the field after half-time, Bonthron stood remote from his associates, desperate and inconsolable. He soon stared at another fatal blunder.' He and Dick Duckworth both went for George Stewart: 'Bonthron shouted some wild instruction ... the wretched result was that both restrained from acting. While they were left arguing the point Stewart dashed forward and easily drove the ball past the charging but quite hopeless custodian.' City 3, United 0.

United's followers were now no longer confident of their First League prospects, but the cavalry was on the horizon. The suspensions of the Manchester City players would end after Christmas. Moralists advocated giving these 'naughty boys' the cold shoulder. Instead, a 'modern slave market', selling proven champions and Cup winners, attracted clubs 'like bluebottles to a treacle jar'. The 'found outs' included Herbert Burgess,

England's current full-back, who started with Glossop at five shillings a week and took it hard when the bonuses stopped: 'Eh, but it was a time of darkness right enough.' The clubs sympathised – they have 'metaphorically fallen on the miscreants' shoulders and wept' – and then the bargaining started. 'So-and-so would not nibble unless he received a good round sum for signing, unless his fine was paid, unless his furniture was removed free of cost.'

There was briefly another stir. City sold Burgess to Everton, but he went missing. When he re-emerged, Manchester United had got him, and City accepted a marginally higher transfer fee. The inevitable Football League inquiry awarded the £68 5s 9d difference in the fee City received to the Manchester and Salford Indian Mutiny and Crimean War Veterans Association. When the dust settled, United's cavalry was in sight – Herbert Burgess; Billy Meredith, football's superstar, back after a suspension of eighteen months; his 'feeder' Jimmy Bannister; and his minder, combative Sandy Turnbull.

As ever Billy Meredith, 'like a giant among glove puppets,' had kept everyone dangling. City's nightmare began in April 1905 when Meredith tried to pull the strings on the League Championship, offering a bribe to Aston Villa's captain Alec Leake. Leake, a notorious jester, thought it a joke, but matters soon turned serious. Meredith got suspended, but still wanted City to pay him. This discovery exposed widespread illegal payments, and almost everyone got suspended. Joke or serious, the scandal cost City a team and then some. Meredith's resistance continued even then. He had always been angry about the imposition of the maximum wage, and now he was angrier about losing eighteen months' earnings. He was also acutely anxious about getting the most out of his limited time left. At 32 years, Meredith needed a good deal. He could not go back to City, yet his best chance of a lump sum had been the benefit his long service merited. City initially transfer-listed Meredith at a modest £500, then mysteriously, granted him a free transfer. Why? City seemed to lose a big transfer fee, and Meredith seemed to lose a £500 benefit, just for the £10 signing on rule. It was an open secret that Meredith received a significant payment from United's J H Davies.

With the cavalry's arrival, three supplanted United men were transferred to Scotland. For someone like Dick, the threat of disappearing into the ranks of the also-rans, even the unemployed, was both real, and a poetically imagined one: 'I would like to read the feelings of the Clayton professionals who, like lay figures in a tailor's shop window, are now no longer deemed worthy of a position in the front row. They can but feel the indignity very keenly … the spell of fetish fame is alas all too short.

The reign of the greatest hero is only like the flickering of a candle, and yet how madly some youth rush into the vortex.'

The current players had had one last month to prove their value, before the suspensions of Billy the Giant and his puppeteers ended on January 1st 1907. After the derby there were many players still 'crocked' and, as an apt metaphor for United's dullness, Clayton's ground was often enveloped in a 'thick haze of steam' in which the players could not be seen – a contamination from the neighbouring Corporation Electricity Works.

Perhaps Alec Downie was wise not to risk his bad throat in such conditions, but it had serious consequences. At last, Dick Duckworth was back in his own position – right-half. And Manchester United won 3-0, courtesy of two great goals by Georgie Wall, although the first owed much to Clayton's special ingredient – the ball stopped in the mud. United's victory brought much needed relief all round: 'after three weeks of defeat and despondency we smile again.' Dick had impressed: 'at right half Duckworth is most at home, and he made a capable substitute.'

December 22nd was a moment of change, for Dick, Bob Bonthron and visiting Newcastle. Clayton was unchanged: 'wonderfully good match to watch, considering the ground was made up of well-rolled, hard frozen mud.' Manchester United started like a hurricane and Dick 'was seen to advantage in a hot scuffle ... Duckworth is laying strong claims to Downie's position.' Alex Menzies put Manchester ahead whilst Dick's 'keen, brisk work' held Newcastle's 'great front line well in check'. But Manchester United were not yet ready: it was Newcastle's time. The Geordie day-trippers inadvertently expressed this when they visited Belle Vue Zoo before going to Clayton, and asked the keeper if the lions might escape – 'might, if they knew their strength, but they knows it no more than you do.'

At Clayton, Newcastle realised their strength after changing their rubber boots at half-time. They won 3-1, and went on to be 1906-07 champions. Bob Bonthron's limitations were revealed, and Herbert Burgess took his place. But Dick's strength was now known: 'Dick Duckworth holds the record for the most positions. He has played outside right, centre forward, right half, centre half, right back and left back, and I think if anything happened to Moger they would have to call on him for goal.' United were now only fifteenth in the twenty-club First League. They needed the infusion of fresh blood represented by their 'naughty boys', but Dick had arrived. He was ready to rush into the vortex.

At the same time, Harold Goodburn's candle flickered and went out. The twenty-year-old electrician was the smallest player in football, and made his First League debut for Preston against Aston Villa just before Christmas, but caught a cold, and soon died of pneumonia. He was picked against Birmingham on December 29th but told his brother he would rather not have played. He said nothing, and played poorly, as if 'all his pluck' was gone: 'the grip of his fatal illness was already upon him.' During lapses in consciousness he was repeatedly 'talking about the game and telling the directors he was sorry he was not fit to play.'

The New Year dawned, and with it the end of the ex-City gang's suspensions. With it too, new prospects for Dick Duckworth and United: 'our future is full of promise.' It would be a year of promise fulfilled, the most momentous in Manchester United's history. And as United established a football legend, and Dick's career took off, so England's economy flourished in 1907 – 'a year of unprecedented activity in British industry and commerce.'

January 1st, 'indeed a red letter day,' saw Manchester in a state of suppressed excitement. The gates were closed on forty thousand people long before Dick and Charlie, Billy and Herbert's entry into the chemical arena was hailed – 'never has a better ovation met anyone in either football or cricket.' Dick had survived the 'very costly' arrival of the four new stars, and took part in 'one of the most enjoyable games'. Not that it was easy. After a frosty Christmas, a mild, wet spell turned Clayton into a 'veritable quagmire'. 'The snow that lay on the flanking banks had been cleared into insufferable mud on the field, and in some places this ankle-deep, glutinous composition was refined into ochreous waters.'

The main object of exultation, and the architect of United's win, was inevitably Billy Meredith. Despite playing his first match for almost two years, Meredith evaded the Villa defenders in the ankle-deep glue and, reaching the Ochreous Sea of the corner flag, whipped across a centre for Sandy Turnbull's only goal. Villa saw 'the same player we used to know, a man who lies well up the field and reserves his energies for friends when the ball comes to him. And then he generally knows what to do with it.'

United's home ground also reaffirmed an earlier impact. 'Several of the Aston Villa players have been in fear and trembling since playing at Clayton: several men's knees were badly lacerated by the cinders which were said to have come from some chemical works.'

United moved from high excitement to a downbeat Trent Bridge, and lost 0-3 to lowly Notts County. Edwardian England was suspicious of triumphalism: 'pride often has a fall.' Suddenly the half-backs were to blame. The extravagant praise recently given Charlie Roberts was forgotten – he 'has not quite been the star artist he was two seasons ago'. And 'neither Duckworth nor Bell were as effective as we have seen them'. A penalty resulted when a County forward evaded three attempted trips before 'Duckworth deliberately pushed him over'. So despite their famous newcomers the League was beyond United, but the Cup now started. New, enhanced United must do well.

Dick now rushed into a different level of football. The English Cup carried a special *frisson* and its own dangers. January 12th saw the country suffer 'a very bad epidemic of Cup-tie fever'. Gates were up fifty per cent on 1906. Manchester United were the only First League club to travel south, and their rivals Portsmouth were the 'sheet anchors of the South', the leaders of the Southern League. They too had developed their ground, including a ubiquitous 'Spion Kop', a huge pile that was 'absolutely thronged, the crowd including a big contingent from Manchester, who had travelled by special train'.

It proved to be a tie of north/south contrasts. Whilst Clayton had said goodbye to grass months before, J J Bentley took his team onto 'the delightful light, green turf and sagely remarked, "See that boys. If you can't play football on that you never will".' Billy Meredith scored immediately. United 'played a very smart and clever game, and in comparison Portsmouth were too slow'. But the 'homesters' fought back to draw: 'a long time since a more exciting and interesting game was witnessed at Fratton Park, and never before has the well-known enclosure been so absolutely packed.' An official crowd of 24,329 produced record receipts of £1,100 for Portsmouth. United's followers thought the tie was won: 'victory, it may confidently be hoped now, was only deferred.'

The gate at 'evil smelling Clayton' for Wednesday's replay was only a quarter as much, but saw another 'tenacious hair raising struggle'. The visiting southerners were not impressed: 'easily the worst ground in the country ... The only blade of grass that ever grew on it was plucked by old Nick Ross and is now preserved in the museum – or at least so say local tall tellers ... The smell and smoke from the adjoining chemical works were most unpleasant.' In truth Portsmouth picked a bad day to visit – it was a working afternoon, even for the soapwork vats. 'All the time the struggle was waging the thirty Clayton chimneys smoked and gave forth their pungent odours, and the boilers behind the goal poured mists of steam over the ground.'

As well as lacking a big crowd's support, United were without Charlie Roberts – he had been 'badly knocked about' a bit at Portsmouth – so Dick was centre-half. A sticky ground, a treacherous surface, and 1-1 until the last minute: 'a wild and terrible struggle in which nearly every member of both sides took his share. The onlookers held their breath – they could not see the ball, only the charging, scrimmaging players.' Then despite United's 'strenuous appeals', referee Harrower gave the goal. How? The struggle was 'fought over the prostrate body of the United goalkeeper. Finally, he had been rolled by sheer force, with the ball in his grasp, over the fatal line.'

The trippers from Portsmouth, in cherry and pink, sniffed the 'pungent odours', gazed at the steam and smoke, and still hurled their hats in the air – 'to visitors from the south coast Clayton in midweek must have seemed a strange scene indeed for sports of the field.' The small home crowd prepared 'grimly to grasp their umbrellas, button their coats and pass silently away'. The wider collective at 'unlovely Clayton' gave voice to this resentment, condemning the players to 'sackcloth and ashes, for the followers of the United have taken the reverse rather hard'.

But Dick was on his way, to a league win just days later: 'Duckworth who improves every week, was a very great obstacle at half back – his fine tackling power and his remarkable speed time after time.' And then another big game. On January 26th Bolton v Manchester United was 'unquestionably' the '*pièce de résistance* of to-day's League programme', and United's best performance of the season. 'The match was won by the United half backs,' with Charlie Roberts the master and 'almost as conspicuous and as effective was Duckworth, and against the wing considered good enough for Scotland last season'. On the other hand a teammate gave an 'inglorious display' and Dick saw again at close notice the consequence: 'a characteristic of Clayton ... If a man is doing badly they jeer at him to such an extent as to help him to the worse.'

Then United experienced a 'crushing blow', one that would temper them and provoke an unprecedented run of success for the rest of 1907. 'A bright, sunny, winter's day, a gentle breeze from goal to goal, a ground as hard as granite and covered with a thin layer of snow.' Newcastle 5, Manchester United 0. Newcastle thereby assumed the league leadership, and stayed there. Dick was one of the few Manchester men to keep their feet 'on a floor as slippery as a ballroom': 'the ground was like a skating rink, the sliddering of players being quite extraordinary.'

Despite these unfriendly conditions at St James' Park, Newcastle, in their turn, were condescending and frightened by the prospect of further games at Clayton, and noted that United's directors 'were on the prowl for a new wigwam – and not before time. Their own players may be steam-proof, and proof against the vile smells from those demnition chemical works, but visiting players are often made downright ill through the pungent smells that infest the Clayton enclosure ... The chemical stench that permeates the whole place.'

Dick's next opponents, Stoke, complained about Clayton's other characteristic, its shockingly muddy condition – they said it was like playing mud-polo: indeed it was wondered whether Clayton had ever been worse. But the match bestowed its 'chief honours on Duckworth'. Despite the conditions, Dick dominated his side of the field 'with almost ridiculous completeness' and provided further confirmation of his emergence. 'One man on our side fairly revelled in the mud, and that was Duckworth and during the first half he made the Stoke left wing look particularly weak.'

Next Blackburn were 'routed' 4-2 and Preston were dismissed 3-0. 'I think our team are playing stronger and better now than ever they did.' It was becoming 'so easy' for Dick, the man in place, the seasoned pro: 'Duckworth has a wonderful way of pushing and holding, but he usually escaped the eye of the referee, and thus his purpose was served.' Against Birmingham he was 'hot shot' Dick: 'it is surprising too, the rapid strides made by Duckworth, and now that he has settled down at right half Downie is unable to get back his position.' However Dick had not yet inspired poetry, as did Herbert Burgess, *aka* the 'pocket Hercules':

'When Burgess nudges a forward
The poor fellow is flattened out
Are there causes –
Not seen to the public eye?'

Nevertheless, Dick Duckworth's rapid rise early in 1907 received tangible recognition. He was named as reserve for the great game that vied with the English Cup final as *the* match of the season, England v Scotland, held at St James' Park, on April 6th. It was a historic match: the last international – extraordinarily, his tenth match against Scotland – and the last goal – his 28th (not overtaken until the 1950s) – by the Hammer of the Scots, the great champion Steve Bloomer. Bloomer brought his Middlesbrough teammate, Alf 'Mr Thousand pound' Common, all competitiveness and wholehearted commitment: 'when Common scored the winning goal he rolled over and over on the ground like a rabbit: he was so delighted … The casualty list wasn't closed even after it was all over. As the Middlesbrough team were leaving to get into their charabanc Common was seized with cramp in the leg, and fairly screamed with agony; quite an exciting little scene.'

Bloomer and Common were the first to arrive Thursday afternoon, soon joined by Dick and the other northerners. The southerners Vivian Woodward and William Wedlock arrived on the Friday. The team stayed at Hexham, in the 'famous and beautifully situated Tynedale Hydro. Their surroundings could not have been nicer': 'the time had been whiled away by billiards, bowls and strolls around the ancient Abbey town.' After luncheon they had a drive to Langley Castle, and in the evening were joined by the Newcastle directors and a whole army of England selectors and hangers on – it was Dick's first experience of the might of the game's governing body, the Football Association. At eleven on Saturday morning they drove into Newcastle for lunch. At 1.45 they went off to the ground and were delivered into the hands of trainer McPherson, who 'saw to their "toilets".'

It was the first England v Scotland international at Newcastle, and there were fears of a repetition of the Ibrox Crowd Disaster only five years before, when 25 people had been killed and 500 injured. However the record crowd did not materialise: 'at the end of Eastertide money is scarce with the working classes, and the double prices, coupled with the prospect of a packing like sardines, kept them away from the National.'

The match was big news, and demanded modern communication: 'the Post Office engineers were busy installing a most extensive system of high speed telegraphic apparatus,' forty experts being on hand to assist the army of pressmen. The 35,829 people present, paying an impressive £2,713, gathered in comfort and ease: 'a gay, buoyant crowd which basked in the summer sun, and whiled away the time in laughter and song with the Wellesley Training Ship band to send forth harmonious music. There were mounted police surrounding the ground, but the fears of a raid from locked-out thousands were happily never realised.' Whenever the bands relented, the Scots sang patriotic songs. Scotland sported Lord Rosebery's colours of red and primrose and England wore white and red, with dark knickers.

The English were expected to win, but immediately the 'very wretched' Bob Crompton put through his own goal to 'the howling delight of the Scots': 'has an England captain ever done such a thing?' England were only saved by their 'superfine' goalkeeper Sam Hardy. The powerful Scottish half-backs 'literally toyed with the opposition' – Ben Warren, Billy Wedlock and Colin Veitch, whom Dick would have to overcome to get into the side. There was just one moment for the England supporters: 'the one real occasion for a full-bodied roar from everyone present was when Bloomer, with lightning rapidity, shot an admirable equaliser.' So it was 1-1: both teams and 'the visiting army of legislators' repaired for 5.30pm dinner at the County Hotel, and soon after eight o'clock they were all making their ways home.

Two days later Tom Blackstock died. The 25-year-old Scot had been recruited in Manchester United's first year. Ten minutes into the reserves' match on Monday evening April 8th, the player made a routine header. 'Blackstock then ran back to his proper position and stood there for a few minutes before he reeled and fell ... the unfortunate player expired almost immediately.' The game continued as United's trainers carried him into the dressing room and his teammates were horrified that, by half-time, he had already been removed to the Mill Street Mortuary. At the inquest Ernest Mangnall testified that Blackstock 'trained harder than most'. He had played Saturday and had not been selected for Monday's game. But he turned up and wanted to play. Blackstock's last first-team match had been the Cup-tie in Portsmouth. An open motor car took his body to Victoria Station and a farewell from supporters and teammates alike, *en route* to burial in Kirkcaldy. Dick Duckworth was a pall-bearer, alongside Charlie Roberts, Alec Downie, Alec Bell, and Bob Bonthron: 'many players being moved to tears.' The next day United beat Cup finalists Sheffield Wednesday 5-0.

**THE SUMMER OF 1907**

On May 31st 1907 war broke out in football, and continued until beyond the effective end of Dick Duckworth's career in 1914. The armies belonged to the Football Association and Amateur Football Association – representing the pure amateurs of the Home Counties, the Corinthians, the Universities and the Public Schools Old Boys Clubs. The issue was the FA's authority over the whole game. The cause was its inclusive approach: the Surrey and Middlesex FAs would not accept responsibility for professional clubs within their areas. The battlefields were at home and on the Continent.

Abroad, the process of alliance-making echoed that between the nation states. But whereas the state of Britain was never able to assuage the rivalry between Germany and France, and thus head off the Great War, the Football Association's victory over their rivals was near total. The FA's alliance with the newly formed FIFA made international football a closed shop, and teams affiliated to the AFA found no one to play.

At home the Football Association ran an effective campaign: it played the numbers game, claiming jurisdiction over a million amateur players. It maintained the loyalty of the top amateurs, who included full internationals like the legendary Vivian Woodward: and kept control of the British team for the 1908 Olympics.

This war affected Dick Duckworth's career in many ways: notably at the end of the 1907-08 season, when the Charity Shield was inaugurated to replace the previous, prestigious annual match between the champion amateur team and the Football League Champions.

The pros shed few tears for the amateurs. The true-blue Corinthian Vivian Woodward was 'in a shocking manner subjected week after week to kneeing, rib-pinching and punching'. Woodward's response was also true-blue: 'Please don't do that any more.' The amateur represented the goodness of sport: professional footballers were a necessary evil. As in cricket, the professional/amateur divide was based on the Victorian class structure and its respectable surface hid much hypocrisy. Newcastle United's amateurs made more money than pros in the old days of unlimited wages.

Second League Glossop were consistent shamateurs. Their owner, Hill-Wood (of the dynasty that later ran Arsenal), openly appointed top amateurs to jobs in his mills and offices, where they got extravagant pay and expenses. For example, S B Ashworth was one of the Manchester City 1904 Cup finalists who was subsequently 'unfrocked', but he had already been disappointed: 'by profession Ashworth is an architect, and his opportunities of advancing his business interests have not been as many as he would have liked. For instance, he thought that the City directors might have entrusted him with the architectural work connected with the extensive alterations and additions at Hyde-rd.' Ashworth wanted to move to Everton, but he was warned the pros there had already proved 'unwelcome' to amateurs. When illegal payments to amateurs – 'it makes the word stink in the nostrils' – were exposed by FA inquiries, players like Ashworth were declared pros, which was 'very like making the professional class the muck heap for disgraced amateurs'.

As 1907-08 approached, Dick Duckworth was an established First Leaguer, for whom further promotion was widely predicted: 'a good word for "Dick" Duckworth, and prospective international right halves will have to be smart to keep him from getting his cap this season.' But nothing could be assured, and the risks of football were illustrated during the summer by stories that insurance companies did not 'fancy' the risks of footballers.

It did not stop either players or clubs risking much at a pre-season demonstration of the American sport of pushball. At the Royal Lancashire Show, Dick Duckworth and Manchester United faced Bolton over a big ball weighing 56 pounds before it was inflated and rolled onto the pitch. The stands were packed and thousands strained to get a view of an alarmingly uncontrolled activity: 'a source of great amusement to the crowd to see the players unceremoniously hurled aside when they came into contact with the big ball, which often rolled over the man and left its imprint when they came to grief.' They played again on Monday afternoon: 'the crowd roared again to see the men taken completely over the ball in somersault fashion, others bounced off the object like corks, and it was woe betide the man who got in its way at pace.'

This season Manchester United would become the standard-bearer for a step up in quality: 'unquestionably Association Football is the people's pastime.' The three senior leagues (Southern, Scottish, Football League) had been watched by over eleven million in 1906-07, a million more than in 1905-06. Attendance records during 1907-08 demonstrated football's ever-increasing popularity. At the end of the season 121,000 packed Hampden Park for the England international, dwarfing anything seen before. In England, Newcastle v Sunderland on September 28th set an early record, but the first Chelsea v Arsenal derby in November established the highest League gate receipts, at £1,625. Everyone knew the First League newcomers at Stamford Bridge were the standard bearers for attendances. Clayton was ramshackle and cramped in comparison, as United glimpsed – also on September 28th – when fifty thousand watched their game at Chelsea. Manchester United would need to match this attendance potential, otherwise the capital city would surely dominate: 'Chelsea is destined to become the hub of the football universe.'

Chelsea's strange history had been totally at odds with football's essential traditions. No organic growth from a community, no evolution from enthusiasts to professionals. Ironically it was the traditional Football League which embraced this paper team, and it was *parvenu* Southern League which, by rejecting Chelsea, did itself grievous harm. The football club nearest the centre of London attracted massive crowds to its 'gigantic enclosure' in its first two seasons, 1905-07 (especially their Easter 1906 promotion decider with Manchester United).

This potential was coveted by other clubs: Chelsea's near neighbours Fulham, the Southern League champions, promptly entered the Second Division in 1907-08. Worse, during this season the next Southern League champions, Queen's Park Rangers, and its most potent symbol – Tottenham Hotspur – both applied for membership of the Football League. Drip by drip, London was deserting the south for the north, and the national league.

But Chelsea paid a price. Even two very successful years do not provide the basis for an easy acceptance of the slings and arrows of outrageous fortune, especially labouring under a mountain of debt. One day they would beat the champions Newcastle: the next day they would lose 0-6 to strugglers. Until Christmas they spent most of their first season in the First League at the bottom, and although they recovered enough to avoid relegation, they had created an unenviable reputation for disappointing unrealistic expectations. Thus, when they let slip a 3-1 lead, and lost 3-4 in the last minute, the cry from the heart swept down from the top-most step of that soaring terrace:

'Chelsea,
  thou trifler with London's affections,
thou football Carmeneta,
  thou pleasure-giver of yesterday,
thou torturer of today,
  reform thyself, beware lest
thou fall lower and yet lower,
  even into the Second Division.'

William McGregor, Chairman of Birmingham's premier side, Aston Villa, was not only Founding Father of the Football League, but its clairvoyant: 'long, long ago, I saw that the two great headquarters of the game would be the Metropolis and Manchester.' Almost a century later, by dint of 'Chelski's' Russian gold and French *je ne sais quoi* at Arsenal (and a move from outlying Plumstead), this premier rivalry was realised. McGregor's forecast was perceptive, if rather premature. In 1907 Chelsea were well beaten 1-4, with Billy Meredith to the fore: 'Meredith is now almost entirely in a class by himself ... The vast Chelsea crowd were driven into ecstasies and were guilty of hero worship.'

**1907-08**

United hit the season running. In contrast, others were not even at the races. William McGregor missed the entire first match, Aston Villa versus Manchester United. It was a Monday evening, September 2nd, the first day the season could start and still keep football as a winter game: 'I arrived at New-street Station from the FA Meeting at 9pm. The bridge and approaches were crowded with a jolly well-pleased-with-themselves sort of crowd. I at once knew they were excursionists from Manchester and guessed the fate of the Villa. My worst fears were soon confirmed. I said to a lady, "How have the Villa got on?" She replied "Oh, Mr McGregor, how can you be so cruel as to ask that question of me." The Villa and their supporters were a 'sorry lot,' 'lucky' to lose only 1-4; and 'all were loud in their praises of the visitors'.

Spectators were increasingly driving the agenda. For example the summer had brought the significant rule amendment that a player could no longer be offside in his own half: 'this change has been brought about by the demands of the spectator rather than those of the player. I have never yet heard a spectator say a good word for the one-back game.'

However referee Bamlett, in charge of the Villa v United game, was slow on the uptake. He blew up a home forward for offside in his own half then, sheepishly and to the crowd's fury, threw the ball down to restart. Fans still had nearly twenty years of fury to go, until the offside rule itself was changed.

United's second game was against the 1906 champions. For Liverpool the visit to Clayton presented 'unusual circumstances' – it was 'actually grass covered'. It did not help – only master goalkeeper Sam Hardy kept the score down to a 4-0 'crusher'. 'Liverpool did not take their defeat lying down by any means; they struggled on hard and often, only to find skill overcoming moderation and energy ... The pace was tremendous, and while the Liverpool men began to visibly tire, the home side remained as fresh as paint ... with brutal frankness, they were hopelessly outclassed.'

Middlesbrough were gaining in class. Their recent history had been mired in scandal and deception, but they won both their games well before visiting United. One of their recent players, William McReddie, showed how things could go wrong when the football finished. William was fined fifteen shillings, or fourteen days, for stealing two plant pots and a cloth brush, and was gaoled for three months for stealing a bicycle, which he ultimately threw over a convent wall. A fate that could await any of the Edwardian pros travelling the country in comfort. Boro spent Sunday in Blackpool, where their star Alf Common committed some misdemeanour. He was fined two and a half weeks wages (equivalent to around £100,000 today) and stripped of the captaincy.

Monday afternoon in Clayton saw an 'atmosphere clouded with steam from the adjoining gas works'. Football could overcome any environs: 'the sport provided was of the best, splendid footwork, admirable generalship, and zealous and resolute tactics ... What could one wish for more.' Common was 'here, there and everywhere', including the environs of the referee who was 'Almost Talked to Death, for the Middlesbrough players hardly left him alone. Scarcely a decision passed unchallenged.' Boro lost anyway, and then, like Dick and all professional footballers of the era, made their way home:

'The team had a wretched experience after the match, arriving at the station just in time to see their train moving out. I strongly appealed to the official in charge of the platform to delay the starting of the train a minute or two, but he refused, and started it to the second. As I boarded it I saw the players come trooping onto the platform. The result was that instead of being home at midnight they did not reach Middlesbrough until six o'clock this morning. The station officials might have shown some little consideration for the team, seeing the rare harvest they derive from the game in increased passenger traffic.'

Football depended on the railway, and was threatened when the railwaymen's union, representing half of the 220,000 workforce, called a strike ballot to enforce their recognition by the companies. Manchester United had time to follow in Middlesbrough's footsteps for Saturday's return, and suffer their only early season defeat. Boro's winner 'struck the back of the rigging as a bee sticks to the heart of a rose'. United goalkeeper Harry Moger tried to strike a forward who was bothering him, and Steve Bloomer acted as peacemaker. Middlesbrough goalie Tim Williamson defied everything United could throw at him. Then an uneasy three-year truce settled over the railways. Manchester United's great autumn was still on track.

'Clayton – in spite of its nasty chemicals – is a very happy spot just now.' From Middlesbrough the team launched themselves upon a series of ten famous wins that forged the first legend of Manchester United, and the reputation of Dick Duckworth.

The first victory was in unpromising circumstances: Clayton was at its 'gloomiest' – 'a dense overhead fog and ground mist prevailed.' It was the battle of the Uniteds – Manchester and Sheffield, who included a young debutant Frank Levich. Frank opposed Dick. In a 'ding dong battle' the Reds' 'hot play … gave the visitors no breathing time, Manchester were soon at it again.' Frank Levich, a son of a football family, continued to make his way for the rest of the year. Then on New Year's Day, he broke his collarbone scoring the equaliser against Newcastle. Something went wrong, double pneumonia set in, and Levich died.

Next, United beat both promoted sides, Chelsea and Forest. In Nottingham, Manchester United's growing fire met the dying embers of the Football League's beginnings – 'for physique, power of understanding and finish, United were unquestionably the better side.' They beat Forest 4-0 under the distant oversight of referee Armitt, the last 'active' participant from the League's first season in 1888-89. He 'ruled the game from afar, seldom moving from the centre of the field.'

United finally proved they were the genuine article when they handed out an away 'disaster of phenomenal proportions', to the champions. Newcastle had dropped just *one* point at home in 1906-07, and were the best side over the last three seasons. Perhaps Manchester remembered Newcastle's snooty attitude to Clayton months earlier, because they really rubbed it in, 6-1. When *they* scored their consolation goal in the last minute, Manchester had only nine men on the pitch: 'the thanks of the North country community are due to Manchester United for the most exemplary lesson given the League champions. Their team of enthusiastic workers – not too clever, but just clever enough – slashing for goal without an instant's hesitation, banging or shooting in attack, fearless and untiring in defence, have given the *coup de grace* to our team of fiddlers and fritterers.' Newcastle were always vulnerable to a charge of overplaying – the contemporary colloquialism was that they 'won't wash clothes' (in later years they might have been called 'fancy dans'), whereas 'Manchester United have a wonderful lot of talent, and it is talent of a practical kind'.

Dick's reputation was forged in this 'wholesale annihilation': 'Duckworth feinted, dribbled and joined heartily in the forward proceedings ... The Tynesiders were broken up by the most redoubtable half back line I've seen in years, Roberts exceeding all expectations ... Duckworth beating even a sprint handicap winner like Hedley for speed. One looked in vain for a weak spot, and given a happy immunity from accident, the team ought to give Cottonopolis its first glimpse of the League Cup [that is, League championship].'

If the champions could be 'mercilessly whipped', a shocked football world needed little convincing that United were 'the great team of the season'. But Manchester United went further: they took their 'insatiable appetite' for goals to Blackburn, a team which had not conceded one goal in four home games ... and won 5-1: 'there is no mistaking the brilliant way in which Manchester United are ploughing along.' The Mancunians 'made their way along the quiet country lanes' before enlivening the gigantic 35,000 crowd with 'their peculiar "war cry".' Dick set United on their way after eleven minutes: 'Duckworth tried to do what Manchester had so far proved incapable of. He tricked Davies, Bradshaw and Cowell in turn, internationals all, and centring finely, three of his United forwards were left with an absolutely open goal.'

It was only the fifth time in twenty years in the Football League that Blackburn had conceded five goals, and this time to an 'immensely superior eleven, whose knowledge of goalscoring is well-nigh perfect'. The United half-backs set up 'two of the finest goals scored at Ewood for many a long day', and 'were in the main responsible for the heavy thrashing'. Dick was 'quick and clever enough' to make 'a judicious and accurate pass' to Billy Meredith who was 'well placed for making one of his characteristic bursts'.

United's victories were so destructive that opposing supporters began railing against their own: 'Saturday's debacle has set the tongues of critics and others a-wagging to the same tune ... less reasonable beings have been saying all kinds of nasty things against the [Rovers] team as a whole and advising the directors to "get rid" of the whole lot.' By contrast, everything was going right for United – nineteen goals in the last four wins – and their morale was noticeably greater than their rivals'. But for how long? No Manchester United player 'is in the habit of finding loud fault with the others. Let them wait, though, until things go wrong.'

United had won eight of nine matches, and scored 32 goals. The only thing wrong was the 'shadow' over Clayton every Saturday, limiting their horizons in every sense. Away grounds could be equally scary. At St Andrews, a 'terrific thunderstorm accompanied by vivid flashes of lightning' persuaded the players to flee the pitch without waiting for referee Howcroft's say so – wisely, as spectators at nearby West Bromwich were hit by lightning. Likewise, thousands of spectators on the open 'unreserved side stampeded across the playing space and swarmed under the grandstand', the police proving powerless to stop them.

United were Birmingham's next attraction: 'thousands will visit St. Andrews solely for the purpose of seeing the talented Manchester United eleven who have startled the football world this season … Undoubtedly the best side in England!' Never before had the ground seen such a 'struggle keenly fought out and abounding with thrilling incidents'. United, demonstrating their maxim that 'attack is the best method of defence, broke through owing to the ground work of their halves'. Four goals in only six minutes followed. Birmingham could not keep up the pace, and Meredith and Georgie Wall got further goals – 4-2. Duckworth, Roberts and Bell were at the heart of everything – 'much of the success which the forwards met with was due to the beautiful work of the halves.' Dick had arrived: he inspired a 'poem' published in the Saturday Football Special:

> 'Secret of Manchester's success.
>
> The half backs.
>
> They realise the game is not played up in the air.'

The 'all conquering' eleven scored another rollicking four-goal win over Everton. They were now demanding attention everywhere: 'what tremendous interest is being taken in the progress of Manchester United.' Their enduring legacy lay through Vittorio Pozzo, a regular spectator who was inspired to coach Italy to successive World Cup wins, and is acclaimed as the father of modern football (Kelly, 1990).

United's immediate destination was Sunderland, where economic conditions were creating much poverty and distress. Nevertheless people came from all over the area: there was a phenomenal rush for compartments on special trains from Newcastle and South Shields, and other excursions from Carlisle, Saltburn, Teeside, Ashington, Darlington, Blackhill, Lanchester, Spennymoor, Amble and Hartlepool. The Lord Mayor of Sunderland and the local MP were also there. The £1,056 receipts from the 30,852 crowd were another record, and ten per cent was donated to the poor and needy. An exciting game played at a terrific pace started twenty minutes early and had only a five-minute interval. Sam Raybould, Liverpool's hat-trick hero against United in that crucial promotion battle in 1905, put Sunderland ahead. But their old anti-hero Bob Bonthron (now playing against United) diverted the ball past his own (that is, *Sunderland)* goalkeeper. Three goals in four minutes and United had won again.

Woolwich Arsenal came to the 'picturesque mud heap' of Clayton, could not match United's stamina – 'the play of Duckworth, Roberts and Bell was really great' – and lost 2-4 on another veritable quagmire. United's record was now: played 14, won 13, 48 goals scored against England's top goalies. Their leading scorer Sandy Turnbull had nineteen in fourteen matches. United led Sheffield Wednesday by six points, and third-placed Bury by nine. Their lead was unprecedented in the maximum wage era. If United could go on and win the title it would change contemporary thinking about the extent to which one team could dominate, and Dick, Charlie and Alec were the reason why. 'Their's will be a wonderful performance in these days of even play, much competition and many injuries ... The chief reasons of their success are, I fancy, that they have an exceptionally reliable half back line.'

Already, and extraordinarily, if Wednesday could not hold Manchester United in the top-two clash on November 30th, the First League season would be over. For weeks the steel city talked of nothing else. For the first time Wednesday would play the undefeated eleven that had won the Cup the previous April. Extra spice was provided by Billy Meredith's statement that United had 'not met a really good half-back line this season'. Wednesday's trio of Brittleton, Crawshaw and Bartlett were thought to rival United's.

Tom Crawshaw, 35, Wednesday's captain, was ten times an international and the best English centre-half over the past dozen years. He described his daily routine whilst on special training. Up at 8.30am to a good breakfast. At 10am a series of four or five sprints, from 100 yards to a quarter of a mile. Into the gym to skip, work with a punch ball, dumbbells, Indian clubs, and a 'developing' machine for arms and legs. A good rub down before lunch – soup, fish, roast meats, sweets only 'sparingly' – and then rest for an hour. A five-mile country walk afterwards before tea at 5.30pm. Then a short stroll, followed by a sing song, cards and 'not too much smoking'. Bed at 10.30pm. A ball, you mention. No sign.

When the talking stopped – 'the cackle is out' – and the 'Titanic contest' began, few could see it. A fog – 'absolutely as black as night' – delayed trains and vast loads of Manchester excursionists only arrived at a quarter to five. Nevertheless, the largest-ever crowd in Sheffield's history, 38,397 (plus ticket-holders) assembled at Owlerton (later remodelled as Hillsborough). They passed notices posted on to the gates 'PERSONS PAYING ENTER AT THEIR OWN RISK.' Even if the fog made it hard to see, 'one's ears told us a good deal about the size of the teeming multitude.' J J Bentley, United's chairman, was delayed, and was found by a pressman 'struggling in the midst of the seething crowd, and very comfortless.'

The referee arrived after fifteen minutes to find three players, including Wednesday's captain Crawshaw, under treatment. Billy Meredith began well, 'dribbling to the flag with a simplicity which seemed absurd, but which had Bartlett and Burton in a tangle.' On the other wing, George Wall was having a fine battle with Tom Brittleton, later one of Dick Duckworth's rivals for the England right-half place. Wall forced a corner and 'placed it so accurately that the ball curled into the net just under the bar. People cried "Goal!" but as no second player had touched it, the referee had no option but to allow a goal kick to Wednesday.' During the 1908 close season there would be an attempt to change the rules to allow a goal direct from a corner, but to no avail.

Now United were 'showing by far the better understanding' but increasingly it seemed the mist must win. Then on the hour came the crucial moment, as man of the match Bartlett scored for Wednesday. Afterwards there were complaints: 'Holden, the Manchester United back, wanted to know who was Holden him when Bartlett scored,' which inspired Bardic adaptations:

'If 'twere so 'twere a grievous fault,
And grievously did Bartlett answer it.'

Alternatively, the fog was so thick more prosaic explanations were offered: 'the horrid thought strikes one that in the fog some spectator may have crept unseen from the rails and hold on to Holden so as to prevent him dealing with Bartlett's shot.' In the press box was Mrs Bartlett, delayed by receipt of a 'bad news' telegram from her father's home. The delay and the crowd kept Mrs Bartlett from her usual seat in the stand, and the Fourth Estate gave her refuge for the finest match of her husband's career.

It turned out to be a pyrrhic victory for Wednesday and their grand old champion Tom Crawshaw. His injury limited subsequent appearances to a handful, and the 35-year-old soon retired to be the traditional 'mine host'. Wednesday gained only another twenty points in 23 games, and their challenge faded away. By contrast Manchester United quickly recovered their equilibrium, not least when they beat Manchester City in what forward James Turnbull later said was his most exciting match. 40,000 squeezed into Clayton: its pitch and fumes at their worst. One star did not want to play: Billy Meredith had felt bitter about the ingratitude of the City crowd in the 1907 derby match and told players and officials he could not face the ordeal again. He did, and the crowd rose to his great duel with City's Jim Blair. Then Herbert Burgess was seriously injured (he never really recovered) and Dick Duckworth fell back to become a resolute defender. United went 2-0 up, and then Sandy Turnbull was sent off. Nine men against eleven. Thirty minutes to go. City got one back, but, ten minutes left, Georgie Wall broke away to score – 3-1.

Over Christmas, United faced third-placed Bury twice. Bury's elevated position was inspired by their new forward star, a young man whose tracks would cross Dick's path on several occasions, Billy Hibbert. It would turn into a dramatic few weeks for Hibbert. First, on Christmas Day, Bury entertained 45,000 people at 'fearfully heavy' Clayton – 'at times the ball could hardly be urged along, it stuck so.' Nevertheless, the teams 'went at it hammer and tongs', and eventually United went ahead. Thereafter it was a case of Herbert against the mud, and the mud won. 'Three or four times' he 'burst through' and had 'the goal pretty well at his mercy, but then got stuck in the mud, and before he could extricate himself one of the defenders dipped in and cleared'.

Bury thought United had an 'advantage in thoroughly understanding what would happen when the ball alighted in the thick paste that covered important parts of the playing pitch'. But United had more than that. They won again on New Year's Day, at Bury's Gigg Lane. The challenge of the First League was over. Even so, 'Shakerdom' was a fun place: 'simply packed with lusty partisans. Right well did they enjoy themselves, too, for the game was a fine one all through chock full of good football and interesting incidents.' The year had finished on a high for United. Over half the league programme gone, their lead was a decisive nine points: Manchester United – played 20, points 34; Newcastle – played 21, points 25; Sheffield Wednesday – played 20, points 24.

Nevertheless, anxiety persisted. United chairman J J Bentley, contemplating the remote possibility of a tight finish in the spring, talked down the players' England chances: 'I only hope the Selection Committee won't take too many of our men for the internationals.' Dick Duckworth would be a prime candidate. A year later, J J became a selector and his influence was made complete. Between 1908 and 1911 nearly fifty men appeared in England's nineteen British and European international matches. Manchester United was England's most successful club, winning three of the available eight prizes, with a team usually comprising eight Englishmen, yet only Georgie Wall (six times) and Harold Halse (once, against Austria) were capped. Bentley kept United men for United.

Billy Hibbert did play for England but within weeks of his battle with Manchester United he plunged into trouble with the FA. In the Cup, Hibbert got tripped once, twice, three times. Enraged, he got up, kicked his antagonist's 'posterior', and got suspended for a month ... without pay. A loss of £16. The suspension was the longest for years, and a clear warning following a recent spate of rough incidents. Often when that happened the other players had a whip-round – despite the fact that without their star forward, Bury got knocked out by the eventual, and very surprising winners, Second Division Wolves. Hibbert's was briefly a *cause célèbre,* one that demonstrated the vulnerability of footballers, not only to their employers but to the authorities.

Professional football was a tough business: David Wilson, Tom Blackstock, Harold Goodburn and Frank Levich all died; Tom Crawshaw's long career was curtailed; and Herbert Burgess started on a long, unsuccessful attempt to recover fitness. Then there was Blackpool's promising King – his 'bones actually came through his stockings'. And Gainsborough Trinity's Fred Morley, who so severely damaged his retina that his sight was lost. There was, however, a consolation: Morley was a schoolmaster, and therefore his livelihood was less directly threatened by his new disability. An Aston Villa goalie had a finger amputated after a ball trapped it against a post, and a Sheffield United keeper was in 'a bad way' as a result of being hit by the ball in his throat. A famous goalie, Linacre of England, received such a blow that surgeons found 'his chest bore deeply the imprint of the lacing of the football on a groundwork of the pattern of the sweater he was wearing under his garibaldi'.

Injuries, illness, overplayed, underpaid – footballers, like everyone else in Edwardian England, needed a union. Manchester United supplied one. They had led an unsuccessful earlier version and now Billy Meredith – he had reasons enough – hosted meetings at the Albion Hotel, Manchester (which Dick Duckworth and all the United players attended) and the Charterhouse Hotel, London, in December 1907. Almost all the First League and most Southern clubs were represented. Their union was founded, and welcomed – as long as they did not go too far: 'there must be no suffragette methods with the Players Union.' Within a year the Union had 1,800 members and had developed new ideas for their future – one was to educate players to be referees! Meanwhile the referees were forming their own union, with Arthur Conan Doyle, creator of Sherlock Holmes, as patron.

The Liberal government gave the union a new weapon: the Workmen's Compensation Act, providing payments for industrial injuries. Did the professional footballer qualify, and if so, which ones? Titled gentlemen throughout the land resigned their presidencies of local clubs for fear of unlimited liability. The 'merest ignoramus' knew that hundreds of clubs paid players small sums. What if the butcher, paid 'half a crown' for his football, broke his leg and sought compensation from clubs whose funds were 'a mere bagatelle?'

The real professional and his Players' Union attracted mixed feelings. There was always resentment towards those who could make a living out of the game. Were the players becoming too big for their boots? So big they threatened the clubs to whom the fans give their true support; or too big for the fans who 'paid' their wages? Or did the pro symbolise resistance to industrial slavery? 'He has as much freedom as the nigger used to have before Uncle Tom's call to arms knocked the manacles off his limbs and made it safe for him to say he had a soul of his own ... I am sometimes amazed at the power the club has secured over the individual ... Directly a player affixes his signature to a certain document he becomes the bond slave of his employers.'

The test would come: a football war was on the horizon.

Clayton. Under its chemically-challenged skies,
Portsmouth scored a late winner in the Cup, 1908

Early Goals. United's great autumn started with George Wall and Billy Meredith each scoring goals against Villa's England goalkeeper Billy George

Sheffield Wednesday, 1907. This Cup-winning eleven did not reappear until their top-two league game with Manchester United in November 1907

# Invasion of Sheffield.

THE FOOTBALL ENTHUSIAST ABROAD.

Invasion of Sheffield. Manchester United's visit was eagerly awaited, but on the day fog shrouded the steel city

MORE GREAT FEATS WANTED!

STOPPING HIS LITTLE GALLOP!

United's Rare Defeats in 1907-08 made news. [Top] Fulham's Cup win was hailed as a Great Feat, even in Sunderland. [Bottom] Sheffield Wednesday briefly halted all-conquering United's gallop to the Championship

England Rival. For years Dick Duckworth challenged Tom Brittleton, here captured in an intriguing stance, to succeed Ben Warren as England's right-half

**MEREDITH'S TOY.**

**UNION v. ASSOCIATION.**

Boy's Toy? Critics presented the new Players' Union as either Billy Meredith's creature, or a threat to sport

CHAPTER FIVE

# SENT OFF, HE REFUSED TO GO – 1908: YEAR OF REACTION

In January 1908 Manchester United were invincible. Twenty-one out of 38 League games completed, only six points dropped, they led second-placed Newcastle – who had already played 23 matches – by eight points. 57 goals scored, only 24 conceded. It was a dominance that had not been seen in the League for a decade, since Aston Villa's 1897 double winners. 1908 started equally well: 'among our half backs where our greatest strength lay, Duckworth and Bell playing their usual fine game.' But the record was a little deceptive. Manchester United had been extremely fortunate with injuries. Dick Duckworth and five others were ever-presents, and three more had missed just one game. All that was about to change, and with it went prospects of a big record First League points total.

So, where 1907 had been an *annus mirabilis*, 1908 would be more difficult. For Dick, United and the British economy it would be 'a year of sharp reaction and almost universal depression'.

It began with injury. Dick missed the next two games 'with rheumatism or something of the kind in his shoulders and back', and United were promptly well beaten. On the following Monday afternoon, he had to play for his England place. Dick had more than a chance; he was an obvious choice. He was a star of the dominant team. Since Dick had been reserve against Scotland the previous April, his main rival, Ben Warren, had been relegated to the Second Division. However, Warren was entrenched, playing in all three internationals of both 1906 and 1907.

The international trial – North versus South, a 'firmament of stars' – was a decisive moment in Dick's career. He was not fully fit but temptingly the trial was local, at Manchester City's ground. Perhaps Dick was unwise to play hurt; perhaps he was suffering 'the effect of a heavy season'. Whatever the reason, 'Duckworth hardly rose to the occasion in the way his friends hoped.' Manchester rain and Manchester mud started to bite back into Dick's career – their combination at Hyde Road added to the 'trials of Job'. Despite a 4-4 scoreline, the South had all the 'discoveries', including right-half Andrew Ducat of Woolwich Arsenal. George Hilsdon scored all four goals for the South, and, as Bolton's Albert Shepherd had just broken a leg, Hilsdon was centre-forward for the internationals; Queen's Park Rangers' left-half Evelyn Lintott became the selectors' latest amateur blue-eyed boy; and QPR right-winger Fred Pentland 'made his opponents look as cumbrous as elephants in a quagmire'. When the England team against Ireland was chosen, Ben Warren was right-half, Ducat reserve. A moment had passed.

The money professional footballers received for playing for their country also became controversial. Dick Duckworth received £3 for the trial match, whereas England players (but not other nationalities) got £10 for an international. A considerable sum, on top of the £4 maximum wage. Too much indeed for the other home Football Associations, and so they changed it.

The catalyst was Newcastle's Irish back Bill McCracken, whose name became synonymous with causing the change to the offside rule in 1925. But in 1908 Bill was still a relatively young professional, and playing for one of the richest clubs in the land. He knew that England's players received £10 so, like Oliver Twist, Bill asked for more than Ireland's three guineas. Ireland said no, and McCracken's refusal to play was such a 'scandal' that 'nothing else was being talked about'. Ireland retaliated by leaving him out of the Irish team for thirteen years: they also mobilised an International Board decision. For the first time, England was outflanked by the other three Associations and payment was restricted to £4 a match for *all* home international teams.

The League championship effectively won, United set out on the dance towards a Cup and League double: 'the cup-ties bring caperings which serve as a foil to the stately minuet of the League tournament.' Others saw the Cup in more twentieth century terms – 'fizzing, explosive excitement ... warm the average man in "shivering times" ... It is a force as mysterious as electricity.'

It was a strange Cup run. The practice of clubs hiding their players away could be dangerous. Plymouth's Allman Leonard was overcome by charcoal fire fumes in his winter quarters. Allman dragged himself to the room of a light-sleeping colleague. Artificial resuscitation pulled him round but even on Saturday morning his trainer found him cold and unconscious. Nevertheless he played that afternoon, suffering from sickness and giddiness, only for the publicity to expose him as Ralph Leonard Bamford. He had changed his name to avoid his previous club, Leicester Fosse, hindering any move by requiring a transfer fee.

In February the economic outlook darkened and Manchester's unemployed began a protest march to London. They may have passed United's cosy Cup hideaway, where Billy Meredith's hospitality comprised a press interview over the hotel's plush billiards table, emphasising the dangers of work in Cup-ties – 'a case of do or die'. He needed the protection of a good referee, but there were only enough of these for the fingers of one hand. A Cup-tie, unlike their retreat, was no place for 'drawing room manners'. Otherwise Meredith feared a benefit for the tough-guy, with as many sly 'trips and kicks as the fancy takes him. How any decent sportsman can of malice aforethought do such a thing is more than I can understand.' So, how hard are you working here?

Well, said Meredith: 'We get up at eight in the morning –'

Sandy Turnbull, who was writing away at a table in the corner, turned round in alarm. 'We-get-up-at-eight! Do you hear that, Walter?' – this to a waiter. Walter grins a polite grin: 'Didn't like to say anything, sir, but –'

'Well, perhaps it was half-past eight today,' agreed Billy Meredith reluctantly.

United's support was initially complacent, only 6,000 people bothering to come to Clayton for the first round. Dick's 'heavy charges' exerted an effect on the hard ground – 'the man who felt himself bump against the frozen turf on Saturday wore a particularly unhappy expression.' There were hard words again for referee Tom Campbell, who had officiated in that tempestuous match at Bradford two years before. Campbell sent off Sandy Turnbull and had a run in with United supporter and England cricketer Walter Brearley, who made 'insulting observations to him after the match in the office of the United FC. [Campbell] also complained that J J Bentley who was present, made no attempt to put a stop to the nuisance.'

Manchester United changed quarters to the Worcestershire countryside for their second round clash with Aston Villa. They 'greatly appreciated an ideal hotel with the river in front and beautiful woods at the back'. The industrial climate was worsening with unemployment and strikes growing, and it was the Saturday of a Great Gale. Nevertheless there were enormous crowds everywhere. 'Football has gained an extraordinary hold on the British people … The most potent reason … [is] that the variety of the game is inexhaustible, and of infinite interest.' A huge crowd at Villa Park saw Dick Duckworth put United ahead, a lead they defended successfully against a second-half whirlwind. Dick's goal was some achievement as 'shots that under ordinary conditions must inevitably have found the net went eddying on the wings of the whirlwind into space.'

And then the Londoners. Chelsea were beaten at Clayton, but United were next drawn away. Fulham had been the Southern League champions for the past two years – beaten at home only once in that time – and they had gone nine weeks without defeat. They were now acclaimed 'rare Cup fighters' by knocking out Manchester City. Fulham had won their replay at Craven Cottage in front of 38,000 – twice as big as the gate in Manchester – and yielding gate receipts of £1,250.

Fulham's route to Manchester United illustrates another dimension to the balance between sport and commercialism in the Golden Age. The selection of opponents in each round was decided by a draw, which encapsulated the luck of the competition. However, Cup matches made a lot more money than most League games, so it sometimes made sense for a bigger club to 'compensate' a smaller for giving up home advantage. It gave the bigger club a better chance of winning the tie, and progressing to yet more lucrative rounds, so they were willing to be generous. For example, United's last opponents, Aston Villa, had paid Stockport to switch grounds: £450 down, half of anything over £900, and all expenses met. The crowd was only enough to pay County's £450, plus expenses, but no more. But had Villa bought the tie? Yes, said some, and the Football Association, whose name was on the Cup, squirmed uncomfortably. It is nobody else's business, said William McGregor of the commercial Football League.

Fulham's Cup run was equally speculative, profitable, and controversial. Their guarantee to Norwich, the highest yet, was presented as a 'considerable sacrifice', to prevent London being without a Cup-tie. First they tried to cut a deal with Chelsea to play Norwich at Stamford Bridge. No good. The eventual deal, like other big matches in the Golden Age, required a shilling rather than the normal sixpenny entrance charge. Otherwise Fulham risked a financial loss on the whole season! Even then, a lot depended on the weather – 'should to-day be wet we are bound to be losers.'

The risk paid off. The Fulham v Norwich gate was £1,080. Norwich's guarantee was £650 plus half of anything over £1,100. The FA took £54; advertising costs were £29; the police took £10 10s; the match officials £6 10s; and gate expenses were £13. Fulham's share was £317, and they were through to plummer ties with Manchester's City and United. However, although Fulham saved their fans the 5s 6d cost of the cheapest excursion to Norwich, they suffered a hail of criticism and abuse from 'discontented persons' at their 'lack of sportsmanship' for doubling admission prices. Fulham swore they would not do it again – 'the game isn't worth a candle. Experience has taught us that although many do not object to an outlay on railway fares to attend a match away, a strong objection exists to pay the same amount to a Club by way of increased charge for admission. As we stated last week there are many people in Fulham at the present time quite able to pay more than 6d. But they could not see it.' The experience scarred. Henry Norris was Fulham's powerful chairman but he resigned, disillusioned, within months. In 1913, Norris would resurface to provoke a much greater crisis – moving Arsenal from Plumstead to Highbury.

Fulham v Manchester United, the 'greatest' of the quarter-finals: Southern League Champions against Champions-elect of the Football League. Despite United's great form, 'southerners regard the match this afternoon as quite an open affair.' 'The air was mild and balmy,' and receipts were £2,160, the highest-ever gate short of a semi-final. It was a vivid London scene on the banks of the Thames – the sun beamed down approvingly, a green carpet, and 'a great, live stirring picture. Four mighty human walls, tier upon tier, the lines of genial, eager, and enthusiastic spectators stretched all around the arena, and to the highest point. Latecomers climbed tall trees and frail posts, and risked their limbs to peep at a game the like of which has not been seen in the south for many years. There were 41,000 of us, and each voted all the others to be admirable judges of a good day, a unique opportunity, and a glorious Cup-tie!'

The emotionality of football had helped society move from the strait-laced Victorian Age to the permissive Edwardian era: 'when a man feels himself moved, I love to hear him let himself go. Repression is death; expression is life.' Now 'his blood ran faster as he watched the splendidly executed manoeuvres. Now Fulham were pressing and the crowd was cheering like one man. Anon it was the United's turn, and the crowd held its breath.'

The individual duels were evocative. George Wall's marker stayed as close as 'Romeo courting Juliet'. Billy Meredith's 'mazy waltzes' were so confusing that 'he hardly knew what was himself and what was [his classy Scottish opponent Willie] Goldie.' Initially, United's 'smooth running machine was all askew' amidst 'the fury of the encounter'. A defensive clearance ricocheted into the net for Fulham's lucky opener. Desperately, United turned the tide with 'shot after shot' but Fulham keeper Leslie Skene 'scintillated like a diamond in the sky'. Then United equalised, beautifully: 'I have never seen more elegant and finished movements at soccer. The placing, the angling, and the delicate strength and resource are rather reminiscent of the green cloth of billiards. In company with nearly all present, I was forced to clap for some time.'

But Fulham won: 'one glad roll of thunderous applause was succeeded by another and another, each richer and amplier with joyous exultation … What pipes and timbrels! What wild ecstasy! Harrison was almost smothered in the mad embraces of his comrades.' The 'team of the year' was beaten: 'victorious players were shouldered amid a tornado of cheers;

hats were thrown high and, tossed by boisterous breezes, lost, one long, deep roar of applause heralded the triumph of the South. Rattles, muffin bells, tooters, all manner of strange contraptions gave off weird noises; there was one round of riotous joy.'

It would be Dick Duckworth's last Cup defeat for two years, and the capital felt their opponents' celebrations. 'On Saturday evening, Fulham was given over to mafficking. Traffic in the main streets was suspended and a band played outside the Town Hall.'

United's own post-mortem was demoralising: 'somehow we lost nerve in that match. We started shakily and never recovered. We had chance after chance ... made blunder after blunder. From that time to the end of the season we were never the same team.' What before Christmas had seemed so easy now became difficult. Before, they had won without effort, without even running about – 'when a man hit a ball he never had any fear; he knew he was going to score. He had the confidence that is only begotten of success.'

United's distress became deeper – 'it is anything but a happy family at Clayton now' – and league performances suffered. There was one last highlight. When United, after eleven straight wins, lost their perfect home record to Newcastle, Clayton could not cope with the 45,000 throng. The crowd quickly swarmed over the pitch and stopped play. Fortunately, football's best teams provided the 'finest exhibition': 'the United Forces. Bless 'Em. May they always play as well, as cleanly, and as vivacious and virile football.' Dick himself remained 'speedy and virile' in the draw that maintained United's title grip. It was an extraordinary dominance in an otherwise equal League – two thirds of the season gone, United had 39 points, Newcastle and Wednesday had 32, and the remaining seventeen clubs were so equal they were covered by just six points.

The League was effectively won, but the season had ten weeks to run: a problem of motivation. United faced 'depressing climatic conditions' when losing 4-7 at Liverpool. The value for money they provided 8,000 brave souls served only to fuel their own financial frustrations: 'eleven goals for sixpence!' United's players were also losing patience with their chemical home: only a promise of a new ground by Christmas would 'pave the way for peace'. United tried everything: how about a fan in the dressing-room to keep the noxious fumes at bay? Only with such promises was manager Ernest Mangnall able to persuade the players to sign on for 1908-09. Mangnall himself had a more tangible reward – another £1 a week, and a £100 'grant' – but no financial bonuses were permissible for players ... even for winning the championship. The maximum wage was £4, and nothing else.

United's players and supporters fell out of love with each other. Three home defeats persuaded journalists that the players were 'not playing to win'. Their crowd was enraged, and their criticisms 'incensed the players'. It came to a head on April 11th. United arrived at 'grassless Clayton' on the brink of the championship, six matches to go and only one point needed. Visiting Notts County were almost certain to be relegated. United played languidly despite Clayton's protests. Late on, the referee gave a penalty for an offence that enraged the pro more than any other – 'unintentional handling'. County vigorously protested. Nobody wanted to take it. Sheepish, not bothered, or – a penalty for the championship – scared? Georgie Wall took the poisoned chalice and 'banged the leather into the boards outside Iremonger's right post. Several *Notts players shook Wall's hand* (emphasis in the original) with unrestrained cordiality.

'One would not like to go so far as to say that Wall did not try to score, but it looked very much like it.' Chivalry, or bungling? The disgusted crowd switched sides, and urged on United's opponents. The whole episode had a very significant effect on neighbours Bolton. For, in the last minute, Notts scored. Rejuvenated, County won at Bolton, which meant if they could beat Chelsea they were safe, and they did – because of a penalty so disputed that the Stamford Bridge crowd attacked the referee! Wanderers went down.

Ironically, on April 22nd Bolton had dropped a vital point against United when they were awarded a penalty … and George Stacey scored! Worse, the day Georgie Wall disdained a penalty for the title, the Wanderers had done United a favour: they beat Sheffield Wednesday and handed them the championship on a plate. Manchester United had walked backwards into the title – 36 points had come from their first 21 games, when Dick and others were ever-present: only sixteen were gathered in their final seventeen – and it was still a record total.

The end of the season was exhausting. United played six matches between April 17th and Monday April 27th. By Friday, May 1st they were in Paris, on their way to conquer Europe.

### The Summer of 1908

Sixty years before first becoming Champions of Europe, and 91 years before their second triumph, Manchester United invaded the Continent. And like later trips, it served many purposes. A bonus for one. If the players could not be given monetary rewards for a championship, there were rewards in kind. A Continental holiday of the kind that Dick Duckworth and his teammates now enjoyed was worth £50-60, with 'lavish hospitality' on top. The club also tried a little money-making hustle. Initially tourism predominated. A couple of days in Paris, with no game, then Zurich, where manager Ernest Mangnall was offered sufficient inducement to … 'arrange a match'. The pre-arranged schedule started on May 9th, when they played three games in four days in Prague, and where they felt the first crowd troubles. United players were defended by mounted police with drawn swords against an 'ugly rush'. Afterwards, in landaus *en route* to their hotel, 'a wild and apparently uncivilised mob did all they possibly could to maim us.' However their rain of stones and brickbats was a lesser evil compared to 'a howling mob who made no secret of carrying revolvers and daggers'.

Then on to Vienna for games on Friday and Sunday. Dick's tour finished in Budapest with three matches from May 20th to 24th, and trouble again. United were leading Ferencvaros 6-0 but relations between the teams, the 11,000 crowd and referee were worsening, generally because the foreigners had 'erroneous ideas about charging'. Ernie Thomson, United's reserve centre-half, disputed a foul and grabbed the official's arm, apparently aiming to demonstrate what really happened. Serbian referee Gavrilovic's arm rose, apparently threateningly, and Dick Duckworth rushed in to defend his teammate. Both were sent off, Dick for the only time in his career, but neither would go. There followed fifteen minutes of chaos. On the field, a combination of interpreters and apologies did the trick, but the crowd were unappeased. No United player got off the pitch without being hit or spat upon. A police charge held the crowd back, and twenty malcontents were dragged into the club buildings. United's dressing-room windows were broken, and again they escaped through a hail of stones with the help of a police escort with drawn swords (Kelly, 1990).

On May 29th Ernest Mangnall, back in London, gave his judgement on the fun, the football and the fights: 'all they do is kick, push and hack … It is a rare thing that you find an official who knows the rules – at any rate as we understand them … We were stoned in Buda-Pesth and with the Slavia club … We shall never include them in another tour if we have one … On the whole … unqualified success. The players have enjoyed themselves … We visited Innsbruck too and have played in France, Germany, Austria, Belgium and Switzerland, and have been just a month away.'

Not everyone and not everything got back so quickly. J J Bentley's battle was in Vienna. The city captured the tumult in Central Europe. On the surface, established authority, Emperor Franz Josef's Jubilee, was being celebrated. Underneath lay fear and resentment. The British were alarmed by the visit of the German princes, led by the Kaiser, reviving the spectre of a pan-Germanic empire. Yet the current Empire was disintegrating in its moment of jubilation. The Magyars, the Bulgars and the Czechs were all offended by the many symbols of Austrian triumphalism on display. Deeper still, although there is no evidence they watched Dick Duckworth's matches, both Adolf Hitler and Josef Stalin were in Vienna that summer (Hamann, B 1999). When the rest of United's party moved on, J J Bentley stayed in bed, stricken with gout and nursed by forward James Turnbull. On recovery, he presented Turnbull with a handsome gold watch inscribed 'Grateful recollections, Vienna 1908. To J Turnbull from J J Bentley'.

Meanwhile a Central European was beginning the football memorabilia hobby. 'A gentleman of Budapest was very anxious to possess a memento of Meredith and he approached him to buy the famous player's boots. A bargain was struck, and Meredith, shall I say reluctantly, sold his boots for £2 15s.'

As the new season approached, the Players' Union allied itself with the talismans of the working class, the miners, by arranging for teams of footballing miners (like Billy Meredith himself) to play on Wigan Rugby Ground in aid of colliery disaster dependents. At the same time, secretary Herbert Broomfield offered the union as a clearing-house for players needing clubs. 'It is high time that the agents and agents' fees are dispensed with ... It is common knowledge that if a player wishes to push himself forward he must give half, and in many cases all, the bonus he receives to the man who is recommending him.'

Meanwhile the big clubs were reporting record incomes. Manchester United's £15,000 was dwarfed by Newcastle's £22,500 and Chelsea's £25,000 – three-quarters of a million people attended Stamford Bridge in 1907-08. Manchester needed Old Trafford's capacity, and needed the likes of Dick Duckworth to fill it. The union compared these figures with the £4 maximum wage, and the way clubs both transferred men for large sums and discarded crippled players, and started to flex their muscles. In turn, the Football Association eyed with suspicion the Union's flirtation with the wider union movement and its recourse to law. They decided a strategy: they would offer clubs an amnesty for past misdemeanours in exchange for real compliance with the financial regulations. They could then punish players who asked for more. War was coming.

Once again, Dick Duckworth was a pre-season pioneer. The Football Association had approved a match in *August*, unheard of in modern memory. It was the replayed Charity Shield – the first attempt back on a wet and depressing Monday in April had proved a damp squib. The country's mood was wrong – it was the day of Prime Minister Campbell-

Bannerman's funeral. Manchester United, caught between a post-championship hangover and their reviving Continental trip, had hardly turned up, and nor had a crowd. United did not take the match with Queen's Park Rangers any too seriously and 'fancied they had an easy thing on'. They even missed a penalty when the Rangers keeper, 'jumping from side to side, put Turnbull off his shot.' But Billy Meredith kept his eye in, scoring a goal in 'a hundred games ... a high rising shot at a few inches opening ... the ball went in at the topmost angle afforded by the cross-bar and the upright.' But Rangers equalised.

The public had anticipated United's lethargy and only 6-7,000 turned up, so charity gained little. The Football Association was not amused. This was their showpiece, a macho demonstration that they would win the war with the secessionist Amateur Football Association. Football League champions versus the Southern League champions – an Edwardian Superbowl! It was intended as proof that the game did not need amateur attractions like the Corinthians to generate a charitable bounty. Instead the Charity Shield proved a debacle but there was a saving grace: the match was drawn. The FA withheld the players' medals and required a replay.

It proved a revelation, kicking off at 4.30pm on August 29th 1908 to a crowd variously described as between 34-60,000 – the Stamford Bridge terraces were 'banked to almost dizzy heights' – and yielding either £1,035 or £1,304! The amateur apologists sneered at the FA's dalliance with the commercial 'syndicates' who would play all the year round, and were appalled by the public enthusiasm. 'Professional "soccer" exercises a strange fascination over the masses, who fondly believe that they become sportsmen by furnishing the means for gladiators to do their sport as entertainment.' The FA's timing was better and United's keenness matched the times: 'the public are fairly thirsting for football just now ... that's what we want in our football – we want fellows itching to be at it.'

This time QPR's commitment was doubtful, undermined by the club's lack of charity. Fred Pentland, a future England international who had starred in the original match in April, had since vowed 'never to kick a ball' for Rangers. He changed his mind once he transferred to Middlesbrough because he wanted, nay deserved, his medal and so 'expressed a great desire to play in the forthcoming replay'. When QPR refused, Pentland paid his own fare to London and petitioned FA Secretary Frederick Wall who agreed 'with pleasure, seeing the match is for charity'. But Rangers played hard ball and a 'great deal of injustice was done'. They had previously denied a Southern League championship medal to their captain Billy Yenson (Bolton's centre-forward in the 1904

Cup final) because he refused terms for the coming season. The players now retaliated by starving Pentland's replacement of the ball, 'as a sort of practical protest,' with the result that he 'was the luckiest winner of a medal that I have ever known'.

In contrast, fortune smiled on the great half-backs who had defined Manchester's championship. Duckworth, Roberts and Bell 'endowed' United's game with a 'huge prosperity from beginning to end'. 'Perfected skill got its due showing.' The Rangers' half-backs included Evelyn Lintott, the amateur schoolmaster who was 'much fancied' by the Football Association at this politically delicate time. He played eight internationals, both amateur and full, in 1908. On this day his 'feverish energy compared badly with the cool dominance of the United halves.'

The Football League's comprehensive 4-0 win carried profound significance. Ironically it weakened the Football Association's 'divide and rule' strategy towards the professional game. Whenever the national league arrived, it was the Southern League that would give way. United's victory 'amply demonstrates the difference in class of the two leagues ... they might have doubled the score'. Alderman Sir William Treloar presented the Shield to Charlie Roberts and gave Dick his medal from a raised platform in front of the grandstand, to 'continuous cheering'. Afterwards they went to The Alhambra Theatre to watch the match again on film.

**1908-09**

The Charity Shield proved that Manchester United 'must have another great season in front of them'. And they started like champions: even better than the previous autumn. Then it had been six games, five wins, and a goal difference of 17-6. In 1908 it was five games, five wins, and a goal difference of 16-7. The run included a decisive derby win at Hyde Road against Manchester City, confirming United's supremacy, and the crowds in Manchester were mammoth despite acute unemployment.

But although Dick Duckworth was consistently 'brilliant', this was not quite the impressive United of 1907. The champions were not firing on all cylinders: the passing machine was not working as smoothly and they were suffering a crippling series of injuries. United saw the turning point coming. For their eighth game (only one point dropped) 45,000 awaited them at Villa Park: 'everything went wrong. Alec Turnbull travelled without his football boots ... one of the horses attached to the four-in-hand fell, and the players had to dismount ... [when] they met a funeral Charlie Roberts remarked "That's done it".' Aston Villa won 3-1 and United were off the top, after *thirteen* months.

Suddenly Dick Duckworth was valiantly holding together a faltering side. He led their resistance, showing speed and control, against Nottingham Forest; and was their best player in a home loss to Chelsea. Extraordinarily, Dick even did 'fine work' in a 1-6 defeat by Sunderland. Such defeats could be misleading: Herbert Burgess lasted only seven minutes in his latest comeback, and United played over half the match with only nine men. Whatever the reasons, only one point in four games was not good enough: 'for Champions it was simply sickening.' United righted the ship with a 3-1 away win and on the surface Dick's timing was excellent: 'Duckworth also did himself credit, and in view of his benefit match a week hence, when Bradford City visit Clayton, it will not be out of place to remind the football public, if indeed such a proceeding is necessary, that he is deserving all the support which he may receive.'

A professional footballer's benefit match, when he kept for himself the receipts of a chosen game, was a crucial moment – suddenly the one-off chance of hundreds of pounds. It was vital: the basis of life after football. The imagery was of the grateful family retainer. The Football Association needed to give permission, which it would not do until the player had completed five years 'faithful' service. But permission was only part of the story. Benefits were 'necessary evils': gate receipts could easily be disappointing – so much depended on the vagaries of the weather.

Dick's big day was dark and dismal, but was the fog climatic or industrial? 'Clayton had a most uncongenial appearance. A cloud of steam from the adjoining electricity works hung over one end of the field like a pall, whilst drizzling rain descended. It was unfortunate for Duckworth, the beneficiary, that the weather should be so unpropitious.' But appearances were misleading. Why after all should Dick choose a depressing late November afternoon against the First League's bottom club for such a vital match? The game attracted only about 14,000, worth only £300 at most, but Dick's reward was assured: 'he had the satisfaction of knowing that his proceedings were guaranteed at £500.'

United's professionals had learnt from an earlier experience, when Alec Downie and Alec Bell were greatly upset by the receipts of their joint benefit. So as soon as they reached five years' service, the club petitioned the Football Association to guarantee £500 each to Dick Duckworth and goalkeeper Harry Moger. However, the threat to Manchester United's financial health from moving from their 'pestilential' home was becoming obvious on the very day of Dick's benefit. 'Old Trafford may have its drawbacks, but Clayton has monopolised them all. For the managers of the club, the question is slowly and surely becoming one of pounds, shillings and pence.'

On the surface the club was generous: United promised Dick £500 whereas at the same time Everton – whose 1907-08 profits were £3,400 – guaranteed Harry Makepeace, an England international, only £300. But his was a guarantee: he was not persuaded to take a match with the bottom club for his benefit. Makepiece's game was against Manchester United, and he made a lot more than £500. Similarly, at the same time the benefit of Manchester City's Lot Jones made £800.

Nevertheless Dick's stature and worth were well recognised: 'it was a fine day's work when they signed him … For some seasons he has charmed the crowds at Clayton with the excellence of his play at right half … Never a moment's trouble to the club, he deserves well at their hands and that of the public.'

As Dick Duckworth proudly captained Manchester United he 'received a hearty cheer all round the ground when he spun the coin and won the toss'. Otherwise it was business as usual: Clayton's 'surface was greasy and it was no unusual sight to have three or four men sprawling at full length at one time.' Dick maintained his usual high standard in a 2-0 win: 'Duckworth was the outstanding figure in the half-back line … The closing stages were contested in pouring rain and semi-darkness,' yet he 'shone conspicuously as the game went on'. Dick was also now a loved figure, and one deserving of all the luck: 'he is a most unassuming player, always a worker, and I hope to see him playing the game for some time and qualifying for another benefit.'

During the autumn of 1908, J H Davies personally directed the project with which he will always be associated – the building of Old Trafford. Officially, the land was already owned by his brewery firm. The ambition initially encompassed a capacity up to one hundred thousand, enough to attract the Cup final from London, although whether the Football Association's grandees, in London, would have countenanced this is doubtful.

Before then, the FA's policemen had found wanting Davies' complicated financing arrangements. Once his sleight of hand was discovered, the high cost devolved fully upon United and brought them close to ruin in 1931. The site was risky for everyweek football. True, it was where the trams turned around, and was near the cricket ground's railway station, but it was many miles from United's existing support, and the club became dependent on an unknown quantity, the sparsely populated areas of Sale and Altrincham. At heart, professional football was something that depended on large centres: 'if clubs in smaller towns cannot command the same support as their wealthier rivals, so much the worse for them.' Manchester United would need the continued success by Dick and the current team to establish a new supporter base, and so survive the change … and hope there was no European war.

Meanwhile, Christmas 1908 presented attractive fixtures. Football grounds on these occasions were chaotic, dangerous places. That day in London, the barriers at White Hart Lane gave way for the third time in recent memory, and all three times Bolton referee Jack Howcroft was in charge. The Boxing Day 1908 attendance was a record and Jack realised the imperative of allowing the swollen crowd over the railings onto the side of the pitch 'The crowd was so dense that life was at stake. A little boy and girl were wedged against the railings by the weight of people behind them, and they were screaming with pain. I got the police to lift them over.'

The two great Uniteds, Manchester and Newcastle, met each other at their respective homes – Christmas Day, Boxing Day, crowds of 40-50,000. Newcastle now carried the distinction of having the world's most expensive footballer, whereas the financial risks of Old Trafford were deterring Manchester United from strengthening their playing strength. Albert Shepherd was unequivocally the most potent centre-forward around – he was 'like a fire-engine tearing across the marketplace' – yet his impact had been limited to the Second Division's small market. But while Manchester hesitated to buy him from neighbours Bolton, Newcastle broke the transfer record – £1,650. Extraordinarily, Shepherd's home debut saw a 1-9 defeat by Sunderland, but in 1909 his goals fuelled Newcastle into replacing Manchester as the League champions.

Manchester United provided more homely features – playing a team made up entirely of married men; and, for the first time this season, fielding the same eleven in successive matches. Injuries and absences had meant 22 players had already appeared, disturbing the fluency of the 1907 autumn. It was a classic in Newcastle, a game 'which old and competent judges declared to have been the finest in their experience'. It ended honours even, each United winning one match, and setting up the need for a decider, which would come in next spring's Cup semi-final.

Now Manchester United's power was back. The 'old firm' of Duckworth, Roberts and Bell was unbeatable, showing 'terrier-like propensities, their keenness on tackling, their accuracy in feeding the men in front'. United seemed poised to fight for their title, and on January 2nd they were only two points off the top – Everton 30 points; Newcastle 29; Manchester United 28 (with a game in hand). Then it went wrong, and it was all Clayton's fault. Not only was it the 'dirtiest ground in the league', but Billy Meredith called it the worst surface in England, one which 'takes more out of a man than twice the length of work on a better one'.

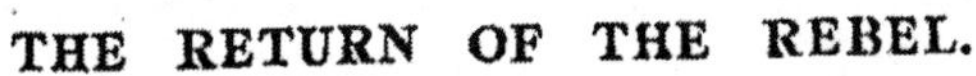

The Prodigal's Return. [Top] Before the dispute, the FA was a Victorian mill-owner /medieval torturer punishing pros like Billy Hibbert. [Bottom] Afterwards, nanny FA had saved the schoolboy footballer from the 'bad boy' unionist at the gate

The Poetry of Full-Backs. [Top Left] Bob Crompton rewrote England's appearances record between 1902-14. [Top Right] Bill McCracken rewrote the offside law. [Bottom Left] George Stacey became United's co-captain with Dick Duckworth at Old Trafford

Ruling Passions. [Top] January 1910 saw a crucial General Election, United defended their Cup, and the birth of Dick's Cup final baby. A reverend said in 1909: 'should a young lady's hand be sought in love, her first question is whether he is a member of a football team.' [Bottom] 'He was to know the game no more' – Dick's last injury

Cup Victory, 1909. Manchester United's day at the Palace [top] was earned by Dick Duckworth's heroic performance in the semi-final [bottom right] and [bottom left] Harold Halse's 'blind hit' against Everton

Away Day. Big games like the 1912 Cup quarter-final between Manchester United and Blackburn Rovers attracted all strata of society

Dick Duckworth's Manchester United Pals.
[Left] Scary Sandy Turnbull, 'The Coiled Spring,' and Oscar Linkson both died in The Great War. [Right] The Stretch of Harry Moger

Chapter Six

# 1909 and 1910
# From One Union to Another

Manchester United quickly lost interest in the League after those tough Christmas fixtures. They played on both January 1st and 2nd 1909, winning the first, but the second was the straw that broke the camel's back. A heavy, tainted mist hung over the ground, and the gluey, sticky, churned up surface held them down ... What had been, so opponents had said, often United's friend was no longer ... Since Christmas 1906 they had won 31 of forty home matches, and lost only four (and three of those during the 'dead' spring of 1908 when the championship had been won). Now the players lost again – 'so tired and so lackadaisical' – and all the wins were forgotten: 'they have let us down.'

United escaped the blame by going to Saltburn on the north-east coast before playing Middlesbrough the following Saturday. The portents were all against Boro. United had scored six against them earlier in the season; and they had just lost a supporter who had flown all over the country with them. 'Just inside the touchline the tiny grave of a pigeon which had been for some time the Middlesbrough mascot ... The grave bore the letters "RIP" carefully laid out in pebbles and a card "In memory of a departed pet".' United lost 0-5, and returned to their unwanted home. Plans for the new ground were in the making, and United's players could not wait to write RIP over Clayton.

Little relief could be expected in the Cup, not against southern opposition – Fulham, Portsmouth and Woolwich Arsenal had knocked United out of the last three Cup competitions. Now it might be Brighton's turn. Nevertheless, both the crowd – 8,074 at Clayton was small beer by any standard, even if it was a wild and wintry day, with snow and sleet falling – and the players showed signs of complacency. United expected Brighton to be 'easy prey', and then found the roles were reversed. Brighton played tough: captain Stewart targeted Billy Meredith – one particularly heavy charge 'into the boards' left him painfully ringing his wrist. It became too much. United held a slender lead, and twice Meredith was carved down as he ran in on goal. He got up, kicked Stewart and got sent off amid 'remarkable scenes of protest. All the players surrounded the official, but to no avail.' Brighton took some credit for not wanting Meredith sent off, but for little else, and United had allowed themselves to be 'dragged into sharing shady tricks'. No sooner had Meredith disappeared than James Turnbull 'laid out' Stewart to even up the sides – 'so much bitterness of spirit ... Very unpalatable ... Plenty to condemn ... Sordid ... Hardly a redeeming feature ... No fewer than ten of the players engaged were seriously damaged ... Some due to deliberate fouls, not a few by way of retaliation ... Contemptible.'

The authorities took the opportunity to make an example of the Players' Union's figurehead – Billy Meredith's first sending-off received a month-long suspension.

Authorities and the football public were also responding to renewed rumours that players were demanding, and perhaps getting, illegal bonuses for winning the lucrative Cup-ties. The small Clayton crowd was attributable to a bigger game in Manchester that day, City v Tottenham. City went 3-0 up, then lost 3-4. Such a turnaround demanded explanation, and there was one available: City's James Blair wanted a bonus *before* the game. The rumour 'created such a feeling of indigestion among football supporters all over the North ... The public are against either excessive pay or bonuses, secret or public.'

Both demoralisation and an unending 'fog fiend' hung miserably over Manchester that week. It was an inauspicious time for City to play United. The recent derby stars, Billy Meredith and Jim Blair, were both in disgrace. United had suffered unexpected disappointments and City were heading for relegation. A 'noiseless' 40,000 crowd saw a 'tame and spiritless' City surrender. Afterwards, United escaped again, to the clear Cheshire air of training quarters at Cuddington, with its attendant attractions of rabbit shooting and golf. Three years later Billy Meredith reminisced about Cuddington. We were never as fit as we were then, remembered Meredith, but there was a reason – 'it was bitterly cold, and there was little to do after daylight faded, and we won the Cup, and were a great and happy side. The boys called it Siberia.'

Then Manchester United demonstrated the new sophistication in football with successive matches against the Merseysiders in February 1909. The first, against Liverpool was 'a game which will last long on the memory cells' for the 30,000 who attended. In the bitter cold, United's stars came to the fore. Billy Meredith was hare-like, 'careering down the line continually' and performing 'perfectly accurate back-heeling'. Dick Duckworth also took the eye with a combination of the obvious, the arcane and the physically unlikely – all at the same time:

'Duckworth, always a fine half to study, gave us a new version of throwing the ball in. Did you notice it? Three times in successive moments he had to throw the ball in. First he threw it hard at the boot of one of his men, and it cannoned back to him so he could punt into goal. Again he took up the ball. This time he threw the ball down fast, the bounce coming about a yard from where he was standing. Hence the ball passed over the heads of the expectant players to one of the United men. A third time he was called upon, and again did he resort to a different mode. On this occasion he varied the last throw by keeping the ball low after it had touched the turf … I never enjoyed a match better … This was the science of football. Long may the players study it and thereby create further interest in the play and the players.'

The following Saturday an estimated 50,000 welcomed Everton's first visit in the Cup: 'the great crowd amused itself by singing popular choruses.' Liverpool's newspapers wrote up the Cup romance but found 'nothing romantic' about United's ground. The cramped facilities required pressmen to be 'living skeletons'; the pitch was 'freely scattered with sand and devoid of grass'; and its micro-climate defied meteorology – 'the teams stepped out into what would have been sunshine at any other place than Clayton.' Unsurprisingly, the locals were 'inclined to be apologetic': 'wait 'til we get to our new ground though.'

The match was won by United's Harold Halse, with 'one of those efforts which players very seldom make in these ultra-scientific days, for it was what cricketers call "a blind hit".' The ball was half-cleared in the air outside the penalty area: 'Halse, who was hovering around that vicinity waiting for something to turn up, made a flying kick at the bounding sphere. As it happened he got a good grip, and though at first the ball appeared to be going high over the bar it suddenly dropped and went into the net at a tremendous pace. The Everton players could hardly believe their eyes.'

Manchester United's run was gathering momentum. The next round saw another chaotic, overwhelming, Clayton scene. 40,000 were already crushed inside half an hour before kick-off under a clear sky and bright sunshine. More came in, and with no room on the terraces, the playing pitch was invaded several times. 'Every part of the ground presented a picture of crowded, swaying humanity, the stands were packed and every five shilling seat was occupied.' Tram-cars were awash with Blackburn's blue-and-white quartered hats, colours and umbrellas and many of their former champion players – who 'wore the Rovers colours with destruction [sic]' – came back for the great day.

But it proved their anticlimax. Dick and the United won 6-1, 'one of the most surprising results in the history of the Cup contest.' But the crowd remained part of the story. Goal after goal went in, and time after time, police helped people over the barriers, including the tremendously dense area underneath the Press Box. So, eventually, that was what demanded journalistic attention – 'as I telephone now, a man is carried through the crowd.'

Manchester United were in the quarter-finals but the weather was still centre stage, producing wholesale postponements the length of the country on March 6th. The big north-east cup-tie, Newcastle v Sunderland, started early, pitying a massive crowd of 53,353 (generating a record £2,521 gate) that had been totally saturated by the freezing sleet since 10.30am. It was a disastrous weekend: 'never in the history of football have we had a day as detestable as Saturday.' But it did not matter: the crowds still came and were as involved as ever. Manchester United attracted another thousand pound gate to Burnley, who had never before got so far in the Cup. Billy Meredith met an old foe – Alec Leake, the Villa captain he had tried to bribe in 1905 – and now Burnley's 'general'.

Dick Duckworth 'was the best of the half-backs' throughout, and quickly rained in a menacing shot. No mean feat as 'during the whole of the first half the snow was blowing with great force into the faces of the United players'. Charlie Roberts remembered it years later as playing on 'a sheet of ice in a blinding snowstorm'. Burnley took a lead and 'hung on to it like Britons', but the game was testing the very limits of British sport. 'Football is a winter game, and I believe that referees should not abandon matches until absolutely compelled to do so; but after the interval the flakes of real snow were so thick and blinding.' This 'genuine blizzard' made an equaliser unlikely, and it was 'utterly impossible' to see. To the fury of the home crowd, the United stars started whispering into the referee's ear, and seventeen minutes from time a frozen Mr Bamlett *gave the whistle* to Charlie Roberts to blow – 'the greatest disappointment was the fact that the wicked referee actually stopped the match.'

It was an outcome that haunted Dick and United for the rest of his career, and changed the way the team was seen. They were now regarded as spoilt, pampered, protected – 'Saved by the Whistle' – and their enemies among the football authorities took the opportunity to add to the whispering campaign. The 'Battle of Burnley' was resumed the following Wednesday. Despite a shilling gate, mills were closed and the council meeting was postponed, 'such is the power of professional football.'

Years later Charlie Roberts looked back on his most exciting Cup-tie: it was not those dramatic London games with Fulham in 1908 or West Ham in 1911, nor Everton's rare tussle in 1909, nor even the blizzard match. It was the replay. When Roberts led United out, 'we were greeted with such a round of booing and hissing as I have never heard before or after.' Although 'the ball took a tremendous lot of lifting out of the mud', there were five goals. Burnley went ahead 'amid a wild scene of excitement'. Halse equalised and 'the Manchester players jumped in the air'. James Turnbull, in turn provoked and retaliated against, gave United the lead: 'great was the Manchester rejoicing ... James Turnbull jumped over the goalkeeper and somebody kicked him as he did so.' Into the closing stages, United leading 3-2, the crowd found their revenge. Recalling the events of the previous Saturday, they began a refrain that greeted Manchester United every time they visited Burnley. Years afterwards Charlie Roberts could 'still hear the taunts' – *'Stop the game, it's snowing.'*

The later rounds of the Cup could excite fierce passion. In another tie, giant killers Plymouth protested a Derby winner with the last kick: 'one of the most sensational finishes ever seen on a football field.' The Argyle party carried out an explosive post mortem on their long way home. A fight broke out. Half-back Ted McIntyre punched trainer Nic Wallis: 'for the rest of the journey Wallis sat holding his face ... he would not have cared if he had not had a weak jaw.' The blow displaced some diseased teeth, the poison released caused a lung abscess, and Wallis died. When arrested for manslaughter, McIntyre stated: 'I am sorry the man is dead. It is a bad job. I have read in the papers that he caught cold, and died of pneumonia.'

Derby also knocked out Glossop, and their players fought among themselves, with one losing an eye.

Meanwhile, the conflict between the Football Association and the Players' Union sharpened. The Football League had hesitated about signing the FA's offer the previous July of an amnesty for past misdeeds in exchange for future compliance. J J Bentley convened a meeting in February that produced near-unanimity – 37 of the 40 clubs attended and 35 accepted The Amnesty. The Sheffield clubs abstained, unable to bring themselves to accept the implication that they had perpetrated any past misdeeds! J J Bentley commented that 'every delegate present at the meeting of the Players' Union admitted that they in some shape or form received payments'.

The threat became more deadly as the FA withdrew its recognition from the Union, and soon required players to resign. If they did not, the FA would cancel their registrations and the men could not earn a living. The FA was also bearing down on individuals. Their amnesty freed clubs to inform on players demanding illegal payments. Turner of Leicester Fosse was fined £50 for demanding extra to sign for Everton. A London paper called it a 'cruel verdict', but the *Liverpool Echo* mocked Turner's rejection of the legal £10 signing on fee. 'Tut, tut! Such a sum was out of all his reasoning. He wanted £100. Yes that was his own individual figure.'

Then Chesterfield wanted George Parsonage to prevent them from having to apply for re-election to the League. Parsonage, however, did not need them, and asked for £50 to save the club. He saved them, they reported him, and Parsonage was banned from football for ever.

At the same time, the union was having uneven success in fighting Workmen's Compensation cases through the courts. This was at the heart of the conflict. The Football Association wanted unencumbered authority over football, and wanted their rules to prevent recourse to the courts. The case that caused the Football Association to decide the union had broken the FA's rules concerned Walter Rogers. Rogers had been blinded by a ball playing cricket after football training had finished. The issue? Was the cricket required by the club, and therefore part of his job, or not? The judge decided not.

Dick's season resumed with his only English Cup semi-final: a Battle of the Uniteds – Manchester United, current League champions, against Newcastle, Champions-elect and losing Cup finalists in three of the last four years. Manchester's United were confident: Billy Meredith said his half-backs would win the game, and trainer Bacon testified 'they are all fit to play for a kingdom'. They sang their way to Sheffield – 'Ye banks and braes' being a special favourite – and found Bramall Lane more packed and excited than for any Sheffield derby. 40,118 paid £2,590 – 'they did not know what to do with themselves and the infection reached into the dressing rooms, for the players were stripping in a state of wild excitement and anxiety.'

In truth, it was the 'worst big game I have ever witnessed'. Manchester United took over from the start: 'Newcastle won the toss, but that is about all they did win.' In this clash of northerners, Newcastle were on the receiving end. 'The northerners were everlastingly on the turn and on severe tension, and Lawrence was busy repelling centres laden with peril.'

At the heart of everything was Clark Kent, *aka* Dick. 'Duckworth was seen playing like a superman, dribbling through all opposition.' Harold Halse scored, and Manchester United took no chances as time ran out: 'Roberts called back the forwards. He wanted them to help the lines of defence. Meredith, sad to relate, answered the call and made himself conspicuous by kicking the ball hard towards the cricket pavilion.' It was the nearest the huge crowd in the pavilion – 100 yards away – got to the action. The authorities had made only the merest nod in the direction of being customer-friendly – they moved the pitch a few yards onto the cricket pitch, thereby creating the only grass on an otherwise bare playing surface. Afterwards Manchester United celebrated boisterously in their dressing room with the rain bucketing down, only to be mortified to learn that the soaked Newcastle side were waiting patiently outside to cheer them on to the final (Green, G 1978, p.233).

United effectively gave up the League programme to stay at the Royal Forest Hotel in Epping Forest for a fortnight before the final. Dick and Harry Moger were presented with their benefit cheques, but not everything went well: Charlie Roberts rushed off when a daughter caught bronchitis; Dick caught a bad cold; Sandy Turnbull could not shake off an injury; and Billy Meredith lost a lucky medal he wore around his neck – he vowed not to wear another before he got a Cup medal.

The players started each day with an hour's canter and a sprint home. Otherwise, the facilities were as at other United hideaways. There was a gym of mattresses, indian clubs and dumb-bells, punch ball, skipping ropes, and 'best of all, as Mr Bacon remarked, fresh towels to keep the pores of the skin open to healthy perspiration'. In later years, as a publican, Dick always ensured he had a similar gymnasium on the premises. By lunchtime they were 'feeding like fighting cocks', and each afternoon they played golf. Billy Meredith, who after 'slipping into a gorgeously red football jersey emblazoned with a white lion rampant', would call upon his partner Dick 'in choice Welsh to drive off'. Evenings were circumspect: the majority of United's players were teetotal but they were required to 'smoke modestly'.

Their destination was the Crystal Palace, a dramatic venue but one in which less than half the spectators were able to see the match – 'so utterly unlike any other place where football was played.' 'The sea of grass, the border of trees, the old switchback railway and the rising ground behind one of the goals, where before the match sailors danced with their lasses, all appealed.'

Ten thousand Mancunians travelled by twenty special trains running between Friday evening and Saturday breakfast. One party carried with them the ball with which Georgie Wall scored two goals against Scotland weeks before, but it was not a male-only zone – 'a striking feature was the number of young women and even girls making the journey "all on their lonesome".' The men travelled 'fast and furious', with music from American melodeons, half-gallon beer bottles and macho attitudes:

'One small boy who had gone to the station in the evident hope of finding a stranger full of sympathy and flush with money, changed his mood ten minutes before the train was timed to depart. He commenced to shout "Play up, Bristol", and despite unfriendly attention, he bravely found a newspaper, pushed it under his arm, and ran down the length of the train shouting "Massacre of United!" A young man in the train however gave him his supper in a rather uncivil fashion, after which the boy changed his mood again; and as the guard's whistle was sounded he was heard in plaintive terms to ask a more fortunate individual – "Corn't to smuggle us their, mate?" He was, however, doomed to return to Cheetham.'

The seeds of the Great War-to-come continued to ripen Cup final day. The civil war raging in Constantinople demonstrated that the Ottoman Empire was in terminal decline and encouraged Balkan states like Serbia to assert themselves. A week before, football had its Black Saturday – the worst football riot so far. For two hours there was pandemonium following the Rangers v Celtic Scottish Cup final at Hampden Park. Goalposts were pulled down and a fire was started. It spread to the turnstile pay boxes and threatened nearby tenement buildings. Stadium officials barricaded themselves in their offices with the £1,400 gate money, and the Cup. The rioters fought with firemen, breaking ribs, and policemen, stabbing one in the face, and 130 people were injured.

There was no comparable history of conflict between Manchester United and Bristol City – except for the tension between two longstanding rivals for the England centre-half position, the two captains, Football Association figurehead William Wedlock and PU chairman Charlie Roberts – but the media took no chances. The Mancunian invasion was depicted in reassuring terms, from both a commercial and picturesque perspective – 'there are no people in the world like the northerners.' They spend their money, and they have quaint ways. 'They bring stone jars of strong ale and sandwiches an inch thick packed in the little wicker baskets which can be used for conveying carrier-pigeons.' But this reassuring picture of self-sufficiency was only part of the story. 'A piece of foul play elicits a colossal yelp from the many-eyed monster – it is a singularly alarming and ugly sound which shows it is an English monster after all.'

The day was beautifully fine after early morning showers. Whether the injured Sandy Turnbull played was left up to Roberts – 'Let him play. He might get a goal and if he does we can afford to carry a passenger.' Everything went according to plan. Or almost. Turnbull got his goal, but United then had to survive with *two* passengers. Vincent Hayes was injured and Dick had to fall back to cover. Duckworth 'deserves a special paragraph of high praise for an exhibition of defensive play of the very highest order. He covered Stacey admirably and in the tightest corner he was a man to be feared by the Bristol attack. His kicking was the essence of security and accuracy, and if I had to single out the great men in the Manchester team I should say Duckworth.'

During the first half, United's half-back line had shown you did not need many other players, 'so well did Charles Roberts, Duckworth and

Bell operate. These men were the dominating personalities in the first forty-five minutes.' 'Duckworth was the hero of the line.' Billy Meredith remembered that his side's early dominance was captured by Dick missing by inches with 'the greatest first time drive I have seen this season': 'the ball fell back from a ruck of players to Duckworth, who took a first time kick at the ball. He kicked it with all the strength of a powerful athlete and like a bullet it flashed just wide of the post ... hitting the side net with such force as to make it fairly hum ... as a mighty roar of disappointment went up from the Mancunian throats.'

The match was 'intensely exciting' but as usual the quality of the football disappointed. Newcastle goalkeeper Jimmy Lawrence, who played in seven English Cup finals (including replays) between 1905 and 1911, decried the unrealistic expectations – 'we are professors of an art may be ... but, with the pianist, he has only to be proficient, and he has little excuse for making mistakes. With the football professor it is different. Whatever he tries to do another man is attempting to stop him.'

The Grand Old Man of the Football Association stayed away – he would not give the Cup to the Players' Union's champions. 'When Lord Kinnaird first heard that the players had a union he laughed.'

For others, Cup finals were an occasion to be seen: prominent music hall star (and football enthusiast) George Robey watched the match in company with the archetypal sporting legend, W G Grace. Afterwards Robey was keener to be seen with the United heroes and fair enough, as he had donated their fine new scarlet-and-white Cup final jerseys. He wanted them and the Cup on stage at the Pavilion Music Hall at nine o'clock as the highlight of his evening performance. But the plans went awry. The team were the guests of another music hall, the Alhambra, and later met some Manchester friends at the Trocadero, before the remnants made a mad dash to honour their commitment for 'Manchester United' to appear on stage with their trophy.

They were a motley crew, just two players by this time; ex-players; J J Bentley (there to protect the Cup); the ubiquitous fixer Harry Stafford, and various unathletic Manchester friends 'of aldermanic proportions' – a poultry dealer, mantlemaker and bookmaker amongst them. Perhaps these were the well-wishers who later produced a replica of the Cup as a gift to J H Davies. The Football Association, appalled at the breach of etiquette, were provoked to such rage that they gave the real one to Lord Kinnaird and commissioned a replacement, our current trophy.

The post-final celebratory adventures of Manchester United are generally described in masculine terms, but back at the Alhambra the players and their wives watched the Cup final on Bioscope. The wives had come down for the match that day, and the night was capped in a central London hotel by a welcome reunion indeed, after United's weeks of purdah in Epping Forest. The celebrations continued: there were shopping sprees on Oxford Street, a charabanc outing to Hampstead Heath, and a visit to George Robey's house in Finchley. United's own bill came to £491. It had been an exhausting and wonderful few days and nights, Saturday to Monday April 24-26th, 1909. And the celebrations of that famous first victory in the English Cup by Manchester United continue to this day. Nine months later, on January 22nd, 1910, a daughter, Ada, was born to Dick and Ada Duckworth, a daughter who in 2004 still lives on the north-east coast.

The courts dealt with other consequences of the Cup final. Twenty-two offences, sixteen of gambling, five pickpocketing, and one attempted robbery. That assailant picked the wrong victim, a blacksmith who was ready and willing to turn the tables and only 'sorry the detective arrived on the scene so quickly as he would have given the prisoner a thorough good hiding'.

On Tuesday the team fled north, not least because that afternoon they had a league fixture to fulfil. Their opponents, Woolwich Arsenal, travelled with them, and joined too in the triumphant procession through the streets of Manchester. It was a tight schedule: arrival at 3.51pm, an extensive celebration before kick-off at six, and dinner at eight. Players and civic and club dignitaries wound their way on a series of brakes around the city to the familiar strain of 'See the Conquering Hero'. A bowler-hatted Dick Duckworth sat up front with a cloth-capped Charlie Roberts and the Cup (Kelly, S 1990). Shop girls showering them with red roses, and ancient matrons waving their handkerchiefs were among a reception party of 100,000 people. Then anticlimax: Woolwich Arsenal beat an uninterested United 4-1 – save for Dick who was noted to give his all – and afterwards there was another torchlight drive, another celebratory dinner (which many of the team avoided), and another presentation to Dick and Harry Moger of the same £500 benefit cheques.

It was, however, a bittersweet summer for the city of Manchester. Within days of that triumphant procession Manchester City were unexpectedly relegated to the Second Division when fellow strugglers Bradford City and Liverpool both won. Manchester City lost their last game on Wednesday, to an own-goal in the last few moments whilst they were furiously time-wasting. On Thursday, United lost a 'great struggle' with Bradford City. There was no lack of effort by Dick and his colleagues this time – they fought 'like lions' – even though it was only two evenings after the Arsenal match. United were motivated to preserve City because Charlie Roberts had earmarked the next derby as his benefit match. Bradford City's win caused wild scenes of relief, and 'a long string of trunk calls' carried Manchester's anxiety. Still, it was thought Liverpool would be relegated – surely they could not win at Newcastle on Friday. But after being acclaimed champions, Newcastle's morale plummeted when they reported eleven players to the FA for refusing to re-sign on the maximum wage. So Liverpool pulled off an unexpected win, saved themselves and sent City down. The ironies were not appreciated: Manchester United had won the Football Association's Challenge Cup, but Manchester City blamed the same body for their own relegation, because of that punishment back in 1906 – 'the City club had their team taken from them by the Football Association.'

**The Summer of 1909**

Dick Duckworth had his own reversal of fortune. Within a week of accepting the cheers of 100,000 people with his captain, Charlie Roberts, they stood almost alone. Roberts later said 'I'll never forget the summer of 1909 as long as I live'. Manchester United were a club divided at its heart. Their players led the relaunched Players' Union: Charlie Roberts was chairman, Billy Meredith was the founder, and goalkeeper Herbert Broomfield was the luckless and ultimately victimised secretary. However, United's chairman, establishment figurehead J J Bentley, was part of the FA Council that suspended the union officials (that is, United players) and threatened to cancel players' registrations if they did not resign.

By July things looked bad for the union's supporters. A fire at Billy Meredith's shop preceded bankruptcy proceedings and he resigned from the union's management committee. The authorities kept up the pressure: on the club by confirming the record fine imposed for fielding under-strength League sides running up to the final; and on their players by deferring United's application to pay Dick Duckworth and the others £20 each as a present for winning the Cup.

The FA Council claimed victory in the dispute when a thousand players resigned from the Players' Union. True, there were many who said they only did so to get their summer wages and would return in the autumn, but it suggested little resolution on the players' side. Charlie Roberts rejected such equivocation. He called a meeting of the Manchester-based players and shouted from the rooftops that they were standing by the union. As it turned out they were alone, and therefore ten Manchester United players were the only ones suspended. The gesture was admired as a brave step – 'they are sacrificing £4 a week for the sake of fighting what they regard as a principle.'

There were players like Dick Duckworth who were expecting a new child, and others like Charlie Roberts who was placing his benefit in serious jeopardy. Manchester United were also in difficulty: like City three years previously they were losing a team to the Football Association for the new season, and they were mortgaging the future to build a massive new ground. J J Bentley made clear where his loyalties lay:

'Manchester United may suffer, but the Football Association will win.' At heart the footballers were fighting the same battle as other Edwardian workers. At one level it was masters – the clubs and the Football Association – against servants. At another it was Capital against Labour and the battlefield was the new Liberal legislation, the Workmen's Compensation Act, which provided the possibility of compensation for injured players.

Application remained difficult. The Football Association continued to assert footballers were sportsmen, who just happened to get paid. In mid-July Herbert Broomfield paid personally for another test case and was in Croydon as a witness. Two Crystal Palace players sued their clubs for £1 a week. Their employer argued that the players were engaged to play football, not manual labour, and therefore did not come within the scope of the Act. In fact it was not an engagement 'to do any work at all', it was a pastime. Judge Harrington queried: 'is it pastime for him? It is employment out of which he earns his likelihood.'

Broomfield was very busy. From Croydon he was back in Manchester where there were rumours the United rebels were weakening. But Dick and his colleagues met only to restate their cause in clarion terms – 'resisting a demand that they relinquish the rights of every worker … And that they have refused to surrender their legal rights.'

Dick and the union now had new allies, some welcome, others less so. The cavalry was represented by the Federation of Trade Unions, who accepted the Players' Union into its ranks on July 1st, and soon persuaded the Football Association that it had to negotiate. Less welcome was the Amateur Football Association. These schismatics from the Football Association saw their opportunity to muddy the waters and quickly offered a fund-raising match between the famous Corinthians and the Players' Union, which meant Dick Duckworth and the outcast Manchester United men. The wider union movement was mobilising: a meeting in Manchester of the Lancashire and Cheshire Trade Unions agreed to render the footballers all possible assistance.

A turning point came when Dick, Roberts and the rest stopped issuing *communiqués* and started playing football again. Because that was officially impossible. And so the Cup winners prepared for the new season in public parks and fields, the grass of which they cut themselves. The newspapers loved it, and flocked to interview and photograph them. That in turn caught the public imagination. And here it was, too, that to feed the media frenzy Charlie Roberts coined the title, The Outcasts FC, to identify the rebels for ever.

The newspaper attention helped Herbert Broomfield and the FTU secretary Appleton as they travelled the country in mid-August to persuade the players of other leading clubs to rejoin – first Newcastle, then Sunderland and Middlesbrough. Broomfield returned to London, reporting that whenever 'the name of the Manchester United team was mentioned it was received with cheers, whilst a voluntary vote of thanks was accorded in each instance for the splendid stand they had made'. In Manchester the United reserves rejoined the union, and only Halse, Hayes and Stacey of the first team were not now members. It is perhaps not surprising that Harold Halse found it difficult to commit himself to collective action: he was later described as 'one of the most dissatisfied little chaps' ever come across.

The dispute picked up pace as clubs like Manchester United got nervous – advertising for season tickets (for both Clayton *and* Old Trafford) with few takers: 'here we are on the verge of the season ... We can't sell season tickets.' The Liverpool clubs rejoined the union, and Broomfield was in Sheffield, then Birmingham, then Bradford. The spooked Football Association finally met with the Players' Union and the Federation of Trade Unions on August 24th. A possible deal failed over the outcasts. The FA refused to reinstate the suspended rebels and allow Manchester United to repay them £28 (their seven weeks summer pay). No back money for Dick, therefore the dispute went on. The Football Association and Football League then outmanoeuvred the union ... they invited each club to send a representative to a meeting in Birmingham where the authorities could talk directly to the players. The Football League was sceptical ... they prepared to put the season back by a month.

The Federation of Trade Unions saw the danger signs and warned the players against any soft-soaping: 'if it is to be war – war to the death. The telegram which I issued this afternoon is the fiery cross sent out to gather the forces together.'

In London on Friday August 27th, 150 London players unanimously rejoined the union, and on Saturday Dick and the outcasts met with the club. They had no grievance with them, they said, and the secretary postponed Wednesday's match with Bradford City. On Sunday night, Dick attended a meeting of 200 Lancastrian players. At last 24 Manchester City men came on board, and an England player – either goalkeeper Sam

Hardy or United's Georgie Wall – denied earlier reports that Herbert Broomfield had asked the team not to play the Scotland game (the nearest threat to an international strike until the Rio Ferdinand saga in 2003). The meeting ended with a vote of thanks to Manchester United 'amid a scene of wild enthusiasm'. But on Tuesday in Birmingham, Charles Clegg, the 'Bismarck of the Football Association', spoke first, and Newcastle's Colin Veitch responded. Then it became confused and ended in a truce: the players would start the season on the assumption that the FA would look sympathetically at their grievances (Harding, J 1991).

The effective end of the dispute came with shocking and bewildering suddenness. But the ramifications continued for months, and for Dick and Manchester United it was difficult to know how much of their disappointments were due to misfortune, and how much conspiracy. It became an autumn of paranoia.

It was profoundly frustrating. After United had led the challenge to the football authorities, there were excuses for the team to lack focus and practice. Yet the day after the Birmingham meeting United beat Bradford City in a hastily rearranged match at 5.30pm on Wednesday, September 1st. There were only 10,000 present but 'for several minutes, there was continual cheering. Even when the welcome intended for the players died away, the cheering was renewed in reply to a call 'Now one for the Union'. Crowds continued to give the Outcasts a 'grand reception' and by September 6th they were top of the League, having won their first three matches. Then paranoia.

**1909-10**

Dick Duckworth and Manchester United had two firsts: the first First Division opponents of Tottenham Hotspur (watched by 35,000 people) and the first match in front of the remodelled White Hart Lane ground – 'the greatest and best appointed grandstand in England.' Dick would have been more than curious – the army that built the Spurs' stand went straight on to build Old Trafford's. Fifty-five feet high, sheltering 12,000, and all for a shilling! United scored two goals in the first five minutes, and but for a referee's 'inexplicable decision' to rule out a third 'capital' goal they would have been three up. Then the referee gave two penalties and United dropped their first point of the season.

Billy Meredith was the last player to come back after the summer dispute, and Dick showed him the way against Preston: 'Duckworth beat Dawson in midfield in great fashion, earning a round of applause.' Dick's effort set up a George Wall shot against the post, and the rebound went just over. It was becoming like that: Preston got an undeserved equaliser, and United were 'terribly disappointed' by the refereeing. Dick injured his ankle, and missed United's first defeat the following week when they were 'bustled off their game'.

Dick was back for the first big clash of the season, Manchester United – at full strength for the first time – versus Newcastle, but it was very nearly the first victim of a football strike. Colin Veitch was now not only Newcastle's captain, but the Players' Union's moderate new leader. On August 30th he had persuaded professional footballers of the Football Association's good intentions, and thus to back down from their dispute; on October 3rd he had to do the same with 'the Outcasts' themselves.

Veitch's own confidence must have been dented the previous day in London when he attended the Football Association to conclude a settlement. For, surprise, surprise, no deal. Veitch was denied a meeting with their Council: instead he was invited to submit his proposals and told the price of any settlement was disaffiliation from the Federation of Trade Unions. Oh, and just to rub it in, permission was refused for his predecessor Charlie Roberts to take his benefit in the next day's match with Newcastle – because the dispute was not over! The match would have been worth over £800 to Roberts. The news preceded Veitch to Manchester and he found Dick and Roberts' other friends threatening to strike in protest. Frantic discussions were held at the Union's offices in St Peter's Square before Veitch and secretary Broomfield finally prevailed on the team to play that afternoon.

So ironically the two champions of the Players' Union were the last to back away from a strike. But of course they were champions of more besides: 'when two clubs who occupy second and third positions in the League table are in opposition, and when those two clubs are respectively English Cup holders and League champions, then we may anticipate a right royal contest for supremacy.'

It was truly a great game, and one of great mutual respect – there was only one foul in the first half, and four altogether. Dick's own physical challenge was precise and effective: 'the shoulder charge by Dick Duckworth was the prettiest example of its kind I have seen for many and many a day. It reminded me that good charging is a lost art. It was done beautifully with the shoulder and lifted Gosnell fairly and harmlessly off the ball.' A few weeks later, a house burglar 'lifted' Bert Gosnell of his League and Cup medals. The burglars were caught, but the medals had already gone into the melting pot.

Now Dick, inadvertently, robbed United of their win: 'Rutherford's shot was a fine one, and was going straight for the net. Duckworth was in close proximity to Moger, and his anxiety to save the downfall of the goal brought about the opposite result, for he kicked the ball past Moger and into the net.' The game ended 1-1 and 'Duckworth, the best of the half-back trio, was cut up in giving away the goal'. There was no real need: 'Duckworth played a splendid game all through, and he was not in the least to blame.'

Dick was now carrying a 'painful ankle injury' and it was only in the Anfield dressing room that a Liverpool specialist pronounced him 'just fit to play'. The game was one of the best contested so far this season, with Liverpool prevailing 3-2. Manchester United's 'really great half-back trio' bounced back to beat Aston Villa 2-0, Dick 'playing magnificently'. They were second, and now visited the new unbeaten leaders Sheffield United. Once again, 'Duckworth, Roberts and Bell turned the scale. They were supreme, and I should find it difficult to express in measured language my appreciation of their skill. I really do not think the immortal half-back line of Preston North End twenty-five years ago could have surpassed the Manchester trio. Duckworth's speed was extraordinary.' Not content with this dominance, Dick was an extra forward, and on the right wing with Billy Meredith and Harold Halse formed 'a human triangle'. These successes did not go to his head however – he maintained a noticeably humble attitude: 'the passes that Duckworth makes to the famous Welshman nurse him and save him such a lot of fagging.'

Dick was everywhere, in attack, in midfield and in falling back to defend: 'one wonders where he comes from. How does he get there?' Which was handy, because for a time Manchester United had played with only nine men, after James Turnbull – in successive matches, a record – was sent off. They had won at their chief rivals, and the 'advantage of the winners lay in their superb half-back line'. It was the sweetest win for Players' Union United over Charles 'Mr Football Association' Clegg's Sheffield United, and Clegg watched along with FA President Lord Kinnaird. The team adjourned to the Imperial Hotel, where Sandy Turnbull proposed the toast of the Players' Union.

Momentum lay with Manchester United, and they won their next three matches. One, against Chelsea-on-their-way-to-relegation, was noteworthy for being a match without a penalty award: Chelsea 'were quickly driven back, and for a considerable period the United literally bombarded the goal. The opening goal fell to a header from Turnbull, the ball having been centred by Duckworth.'

Now United were second to Blackburn, the new form team, six wins in their last seven games, during which their recent goal difference was 19-2. Yet another top-two challenge produced a 'magnetic attraction', the *'pièce de résistance'* of the day's programme: 'I have seen Cup finals in

England, Scotland and Ireland, International matches, and other representative games, but I have never witnessed a more thrilling game … There has never been such a day in the town, and all records of attendance – over 35,000 were present – went by the board.'

Yet there was even more at stake. It was another grudge match. All United's controversial battles had been against sides who had opposed the Players' Union. Sheffield United had refused to rejoin; Spurs wanted a union approved by the FA; and Aston Villa constantly changed their minds. James Turnbull was twice sent off against these sides who seemed to be favoured by the FA's referees.

Before the game with Blackburn the result of the players' ballot was announced: the majority decided to do what the Football Association wanted – to resign from the wider union movement of workers and disaffiliate from the Federation of Trade Unions. Manchester 'PU' United now aimed to take out their frustrations on the Rovers, who had resisted all blandishments by the union – 'the United are making no secret of their determination to put a spoke in the wheel of a team … owing to their attitude upon the fight between the Players' Union and the Football Association.'

A precariously swaying multitude filled even the gangways, and soon the touchlines in front of the grandstand were lined with displaced persons. The previous high stemmed from Manchester United's triumphal procession through the might of English football in the autumn of 1907, when Rovers were dismissed 5-1 on their own ground. Now they set a new record – receipts of £1,178. Dick outpaced the current England back: 'the Manchester men pressed hotly, and Meredith placing forward as Duckworth shouted there was a glorious bit of play, Duckworth making a great sprint past Cowell, and driving the ball at goal with all his might.'

But frustration set in. Two penalties in one match had cost them a point earlier against Spurs. Surely that could not happen again. Then Rovers were given a penalty, and United refused one, for handball. Rovers led 2-0 with fifteen minutes to go, but United got one back, and Dick roamed in search of the equaliser. 'Duckworth, going to the inside position, sent across a shot which missed the far post by about a foot.' United did equalise, and were battling to hold on to their point close to the end. Then followed 'one of the most peculiar incidents I have seen on the football field'. For other commentators, deep into a mid-November afternoon, it was hard to see:

'The second penalty kick was even more unsatisfactory, but I was not in a position owing to the distance and the failing light to pass a decided opinion. Anyhow, a free kick was given on the left wing just beyond the penalty area. Duckworth encroached, and was ordered back, and was doubtless nettled. He appeared to show he was the necessary six paces away. Be that as it may, Duckworth jumped up as the kick was taken, spread out his arms, and whether he had any intention of striking the ball or whether the ball struck him he knows best, and Mr Stark immediately gave a penalty. This was the last straw that broke the United back, and they plainly showed their opinion of the referee.'

The handball decision for a penalty was one that infuriated the pro and left legislators unclear about intention. One famous referee revealed how closely he paid attention to intentionality when he denied a penalty kick for handball: 'I might have been better placed to divine the man's intentions had I been standing in front of him and able to see his face.' Dick's attempted block made it an 'utter impossibility' for him to see the ball, and United did not hide their feelings: 'nothing more childish could have been imagined than the antics that followed the second penalty-kick and the scene at the end ... was not only unique as far as the Rovers is concerned, but might have led to something serious.'

Penalties were a topic because a third of those taken so far in the First League had been missed – perhaps because goalkeepers were allowed to come forward from their line – but Rovers scored theirs. Still United did not give up: they responded with 'fast and furious' play in a 'stirring finale' and 'Duckworth shot brilliantly for Ashcroft to save' – but there was not enough time: 'it was indeed a match which will ever be remembered in Blackburn, and I question if there will ever be such another game played there.'

But it wasn't over. Two unnamed United players (Dick had most reason) left the pitch still arguing with the referee over that late penalty: 'the official insisted that they should leave the field first, one did not comply until Superintendent Dobson persuaded him to walk off.' The atmosphere was explosive, causing 'the crowd, already highly strung, to seethe with excitement. The spectators swarmed the rails, and gathering on the playing pitch hooted the United player.'

Penalties, disallowed goals, sendings off, it was a time which people would later look back on: 'when Manchester United were passing through a period of adversity, a year or two ago, they said that every ref they met was prejudiced against them.' And behind it all, you could not help thinking, was the Football Association, out to get their own back. Billy Meredith had been the last of the players to come back after the dispute. He railed against his fellow professionals' feebleness – they were content, he said, to live a kind of schoolboy life. After the Blackburn game,

Meredith reported 'there is no greater certainty than that Duckworth will play for England this season. In match after match he has been bang at the top of his form.' So when that did not happen, Meredith, ever the conspiracist, said the only reason the Football Association selectors could have for omitting him was that he played for the wrong team, the 'wreckers of football,' the union club, the Outcasts.

There was reason to believe the Football Association were paying back scores. At the conference in August the star of the show was Preston's Rufus 'Ginger' Lyon. Lyon railed against the FA's previous lack of natural justice when they suspended him for months without a hearing: 'I was never in the know, and now I want £113 from the Association – £88 in wages lost and £25 for my fine. I can't fight the Association: I am a poor individual – a tailor, in fact by trade and we ought to have a union to protect our rights.' At the time FA Chairman Charles Clegg had no answer. However, the week after United played Rovers, Lyon played an unremarkable game for Preston, after which he was suspended for a month. The referee and linesmen had seen nothing amiss, but a visiting FA luminary spotted some violent play *off the ball*. Then the FA Council refused to reconsider the life ban imposed on George Parsonage last spring, even when delivered of a petition signed by 1,400 professionals. And then they made Manchester United squirm.

United's discomfort started when, like all clubs, they took advantage of the FA's amnesty in the previous season. The point of The Amnesty was that disclosure of past misdeeds would prevent punishment. It did not quite work out like that. Most clubs admitted illegal payments in their official accounts. In United's case, all these payments were made by a private individual – President Davies. Mr Davies rendered an account of £7,230 as part of the amnesty and the club reimbursed him. All this struck the FA as against the spirit of their previous agreement with Manchester United. Remember, United's financial arrangements were only accepted when J J Bentley, uneasily straddling Association and League, gave his 'personal guarantee' that the books were 'proper'. Now it seemed, J J had been kept, conveniently, 'in the dark.' The FA threatened to publicise United's crimes. United protested, not unreasonably: how was this an amnesty? But they had to submit, and were humiliated. The FA report in March 1910 was the 'sensation of the hour … "'orrid 'ot".' The only named recipient of President Davies' largesse was J J B himself: in contravention of the rule against directors receiving payment, he had been paid £1,400. The FA would not sanction any repayment to Mr Davies, and supervised United's affairs until November 1911. The union club was muzzled …

The Blackburn match effectively ended Dick's, and Manchester United's league season. Apart from a match against Spurs on January 22nd, 1910, United lost five of the next nine fixtures, scoring only twelve goals and conceding twenty. Dick missed eight games, a sad anticlimax after his heroic autumn. The early weeks of 1910, sandwiching the birth of Dick's daughter, saw the first of 1910's groundbreaking General Elections. The result left the Liberals still in power, but now dependent on the parliamentary support of Labour and, more importantly, on John Redmond's Irish Nationalists, whose price would be a Home Rule for Ireland Act.

The destination of the season's prizes increasingly took second place to a project that was much more significant in the club's history – the move to Old Trafford. And the ground offered a teasing descant to the team's requiem as the opening was put off from November to December to January 22nd. And the week before that, Manchester United had to defend their English Cup, and of all places, they did so in Burnley. Dick Duckworth was thought to have no chance of playing, but he was with the squad at their usual winter quarters at Norbreck Hydro. Dick played, but clearly should not have done, because it promptly put him out again until February 19th, and that turned out to be an auspicious date.

Dick and Manchester United received a very hot return to Burnley. Turf Moor supporters remembered how the snow had saved United last March. The veteran football journalist 'The Veteran' was impressed by the vitriol: 'I never saw a team hissed and hooted when they went out to play a Cup-tie.' United were beaten and for the only time in his career Dick Duckworth faced a late winter and spring without a chance of any prize.

To add to the disappointment, Old Trafford was still not ready, so unloved Clayton hosted a last match, watched by 'no more than 4,000'. It is tempting to see the poor crowd as either a judgement on United's lost year or urban Manchester's final protest, but it was not out of step with attendances that Saturday. Chelsea attracted 33,000, three other clubs over ten thousand, but the remaining six fixtures were comparable with Clayton.

Dick was otherwise engaged – his daughter was born that day, January 22nd, 1910. The football gods were in a tempestuous mood. Gales destroyed Clayton's grandstand days before Old Trafford's opening, and contemporary match events reflected these stormy portents. Spurs were beaten 5-0 in the Clayton finale. Then Manchester United went 0-3 down at half-time to Newcastle in Bert Gosnell's benefit, yet came back to win 4-3. The defending champions felt a barrage, and replied with echoes of the Great War to come: 'from right and left have I been assailed by our disappointed partisans, the more boisterous and wilder of whom even go so far as to ask me if the game was sold, if there was some subterfuge that the onlooker was not in a position to detect, or if we fell to pieces simply for want of training ... 'Tis a fickle public we cater to, indeed ... I can warrant all my readers that every man on last Saturday did his duty.'

The week after Old Trafford opened, Aston Villa – the 'coming champions' – thrashed United 7-1, only Dick Duckworth resisting the worst defeat of his career. Charlie Roberts dislocated fingers; goalkeeper Harry Moger – left out because he had conceded seven goals in two matches – saw his successor equal that in one go. For the Villa 'it reads almost like a fairy tale ... Prodigious! The score speaks for itself; but who could have imagined such a thing.' Beforehand, Villa were second, only four points ahead of United. Afterwards they strode away to win the League by some distance. Two years later, Billy Gerrish, scorer of two Villa goals against United, suffered another consequence of the Players' Union defeat. He was sacked, for 'palpable inefficiency'.

The opening match itself on February 19th saw equally dramatic swings – United led 3-1 with three-quarters gone, but Liverpool came back dramatically to win 4-3. At a colossal cost of £60,000, 'the like of Old Trafford has never been seen before in English football' – palatial, but with frills – a white picket fence surrounding the pitch ... to indicate its new suburban setting. Opening day was a carnival. 'A great stream' spread from Manchester, its trams entertained by 'sundry small boys' offering 'twenty cartwheels and a roll-over' for a penny. Thousands more came from parts which football had not previously 'touched'. Entrances were immediately overwhelmed: the 45,000 inside produced receipts of £1,200 but they were joined by freeloaders, 500 VIPs and another 5,000 who 'broke through and entered without paying'. 'The greatest crowd that ever saw a league match in Manchester.'

The turf – 'presenting the beautiful fresh greenness of a cricket field' – suited Dick: 'Duckworth was the best half-back on the field.' His well placed free-kick set up the first-ever goal at Old Trafford, and he 'showed extraordinary speed' on the virgin surface. After that first defeat, United won their seven remaining 1909-10 home matches, scoring nineteen goals, and conceding only four. Dick was then 'the pick of the half-back line' in United's first win at Old Trafford, against Sheffield United – 'the pace of Duckworth made him the most prominent. On the new turf the ball was astonishingly fast.'

But the new home only increased the pressure to fill the ground. On a wet weekend in March, United looked into the abyss – failing to balance the books. The match with Woolwich Arsenal – also in financial distress – was goalless. The old Plumstead pitch had the men 'floundering about in the mire'. Arsenal were second from bottom and in danger of relegation. But the talk that day was all about Arsenal's imminent collapse: the banks were 'threatening to foreclose'. An extraordinary general meeting weeks later was redolent of 1902, when Newton Heath transmuted into Manchester United. 'If any man has anything to say let him say it; but those who have no sense should say nothing.'

Dick Duckworth recovered fitness too late to make a serious bid for England honours, despite being a 'certainty' the previous November. Andrew Ducat played right-half in all three internationals. But there was another route. The Football Association were still battling with the Amateur Football Association over international recognition, and the price of the South African Football Association's loyalty was a senior tour to coincide with Union Day, the effective independence of the South African State.

In February, the Football Association began approaching England's top footballers. The country's premier goalkeeper, Sam Hardy, pondered whether to go. There was little in favour. A four-month trip meant no rest at all between seasons, and 'travelling was a veritable bore to professional footballers' (he reckoned an average 300 miles a week). Hardy bemoaned the neglect of any home business, and the money was, well, no good: 'I do not think the question of remuneration weighs largely with the player … The incremental expenses in such a trip will be considerable.' That was what Hardy thought, but he imagined (or described) a 'debate across the breakfast table' that carried even more weight:

'The lady of the house has heard ghost stories of South Africa, and these penetrate into the nervous system. The result is that after being addressed by your wife for about three minutes you begin to think that of a truth these things do really exist. They paint a gruesome picture of the effects of the fevers of that land, which are certain to claim you as a victim. Then there is the chance of a watery grave. In fact you cannot escape one way or the other the cruel death that awaits you … The wife will play a very important part in regard to the composition of England's team for that far-off country.'

Sam Hardy did not go, but Dick Duckworth did, despite at this point having a daughter aged one month. In February he was given a month's grace to decide, because of Mrs Duckworth's health. What did she say?

Dick thus joined the first official team from England to the Empire. The team received a grand celebratory farewell in London, presided over by the grandest of Football Association grandees, Lord Kinnaird. The 'sacrifice' the party was making for 'the bond of union' between the old country and the newest of all countries was heralded. There were family farewells choked with emotion – children's farewells to their fathers 'crushed the life from out young hearts'.

The Heroes left a dying king and the end of the Edwardian era. Would the new world be 'a playground' for the FA's amateurs? The tour rewarded those university blues who spurned the rival Amateur Football Association and stayed loyal to *the* Football Association. There was legendary captain Vivian Woodward, and a trio of amateur wingers who had each played once for the full England side – James Raine, of shamateur club Glossop; Gordon Wright, who toured South Africa with the Corinthians; and Arthur Berry, who had played for England whilst with Oxford University. Berry would play regularly for Everton in the 1910-11 First Division although his father was Liverpool's chairman. England's tour manager celebrated this quality with the South African press: 'the Football Association, as you see, commands the services of the best amateurs playing, including university men, as you may judge from the constitution of the team.'

But did the Corinthian spirit answer the colonists' main question – 'how is it Association Football has such a wonderful hold on the public in the Old Country?' No, it did not. The South Africans had received visits from the Corinthians and paid generously –£3,000 in 1906 – but it was not enough. They wanted the thing that really distinguished English football, its professional footballer: his skill, dexterity, resilience and above all consistency. The squad was strong, although to the South African public some star names were missing. England captain Bob Crompton initially agreed, then withdrew. Colin Veitch was approached, but clubs like Newcastle were as reluctant as wives to let their men go. Manchester United nobly donated three top pros – Dick, Georgie Wall and Vincent Hayes. Half the party were internationals, with seven other sometime full England players – Wedlock, Holley, Benson, Richards, Hibbert, Fleming and Sturgess. Their hosts welcomed the whole party as a 'judicious blend of amateur and professional', encompassing the personal qualities that distinguished the Edwardian 'manly man'; each one chosen for his 'sportsmanship and cleanliness of life and liberty'. Nevertheless, the pros could be depicted as salt of the earth working-class types. Manchester United's Vincent Hayes, ex-Newton Heath and ex-boilermaker, was 'nobbut a Lancashire lad, but he's a reet 'un' (he once had to have a leg re-broken when it set badly). He boasted they would win all their matches, and the League when they got back. Dick entered into the spirit – "and the English Cup," laughingly added Dick.'

Dick suffered *mal de mer* in the Bay of Biscay and a regular Cape swell on the eve of their arrival. In between they had a scenic stopover on Madeira and Dick won the potato race amid endless deck games on a seventeen-day voyage. The South African delegation slept onboard ship in Cape Town harbour, to be punctual for the SS *Kinfaun Castle*'s arrival.

'Welcome to South Africa,' shouted the Honorary Treasurer. 'Glad to meet you, and hope to see more of it,' returned the tourists. The locals had been anxious about the financial underpinnings to the tour, and welcomed the belated intervention of one of Cape Town's richer citizens. 'The local association has experienced great difficulty in arranging the guarantee required by the South African Football Association in connection with the English tour. Everyone will be glad to learn that at the last moment, thanks to the generosity of a well-known public man their difficulties have been overcome.'

In football history the three tests with South Africa are not accepted as full internationals. The reason is imperial. Two years earlier, an FA side beat Bohemia, no independent nation, rather a part of the Austro-Hungarian Empire, and that is regarded as authentically international. But South Africa was a nation of Britain's Empire, and therefore not wholly separable. Symbolically, too, for its subtext of advancing links with the Empire, the tourists arrived on Empire Day. During the tour, South Africa elected its first autonomous government and football captured the meaning of the motherland, recognising the growing maturity of its colonial offspring. 'England has recognised the growing strength of South African Socker – the attainment of the game to man's estate in fact.'

The players were unimpressed by Cape Town. After being driven up from the docks by brakes to the Grand Hotel, they took a stroll around and expressed the 'almost unanimous opinion that it was a remarkably quiet city', after the bustle and noise of their home hives of industry, Manchester and Sheffield. However at lunch-time they were entertained by his Worship the Lord Mayor, and afterwards a first 'kick around' on the Rhodes Recreation Ground impressed onlookers – 'they look, and are, as tough and hard as the proverbial nail.' England had provided South Africa with 'just the team that is wanted'. A 'wildly enthusiastic' three thousand spectators, including two hundred soldiers from the English garrison York Regiment, watched their first match, two days after arrival, on a glorious autumn afternoon – if a 'trifle warm' – May 26th, against the Colonial Born of Cape Town, played on the Green Point Track.

Sunderland's George Holley wrote home: 'Billy Wedlock offered me £5 for every blade of grass I could find on the playing pitch: 'I might as well have searched for diamonds.' Nevertheless, the gifted half-back line of Duckworth, Wedlock and Albert Sturgess of Sheffield United – tough as several nails – dominated in a 7-1 win. Their 'matchless tactics' formed an 'impenetrable barrier' to the home forwards. 'From the sole of their feet to the crown on their heads they are workmen right through.'

Another modern fashion that had permeated the colony was the practice of spectators invading the pitch after the game, and chairing the victors off. It was something that Dick had experienced before. That evening the highlight of the team's musical evening was the English Cup final on cinematograph; and next day they took tea in Cecil Rhodes' house watching the sun set over Table Mountain.

On Saturday May 28th, England played Western on the same Green Point Track, by now reduced to mud by pouring rain, and in these more homely conditions won 13-0. The most talented home player was Commaille, who had appeared in all five Tests against England in the cricket series that had ended just two months before.

But it was time for Dick and his Empire men to move on, into the hinterland of South Africa. As their train wound its way round and round twelve times up one thousand feet out of Cape Town, he may have read *The Cape Times'* special supplement on the Cape Government Railways. It was a special day: in many ways it was the end of Empire in South Africa. A newly elected federal government took over the administration. Apartheid was on its way. It was Union Day.

Fickle Judgements. At first cartoonists sympathised with the players, but soon thought they were becoming over-mighty

Golden Personalities. [Top] Charlie Thomson's fearsome appearance made him an Edwardian Mephistopheles, but he acted the angel in The Affair of the Colonel's Bribe. [Right] Notts County's Iremonger, equally terrifying, was 'tall enough to light his cigarette at a lamppost'. [Bottom] Who had the last laugh? Villa captain Alec Leake snitched on Billy Meredith in the 1905 bribe scandal, then skippered Burnley, whom United robbed in the 1909 Cup quarter-final

SHADOWS SEEKING FOR SUBSTANCE.

Manchester United Alone. [Top] Crunch-time came when the FA heavies put the squeeze on, requiring pros to sign a new registration form or lose their livelihood. United were left alone for the never-to-be-forgotten summer of 1909. [Bottom] By the autumn, United were afflicted by the shadows of paranoia

The Penalty. The FA's best (Mr Stark refereed the 1909 England v Scotland game) gave Blackburn Rovers victory over The Outcasts

Images of Empire. [Top] Dick Duckworth and the FA's 'tip top Englishmen' were 'peaceful footballers' when they embarked for post-Boer War South Africa, and sharpshooters when they arrived. [Bottom] Soccer Test wins made up for losses by England's cricket and rugby tourists earlier in 1910

Chapter Seven

# 1910-11
# Old Trafford's Championship

The journey through South Africa was redolent, more than anything else, of the event to which the Golden Age referred again and again – the Boer War. They passed hundreds of soldier graves of General French's forced march across the veldt – the same general would send thousands and thousands more to unmarked graves in the Great War. After a thirty-hour, 700-mile train journey the tourists reached the diamond capital of Kimberley, where, 2,520 feet down a mine, they bade 'Goodbye to England if the engine-driver makes a slip'. (When they were in the East Rand, 'one white man and 28 natives' died in a local gold mine fire.) Off again to Griqualand West, and the site where the Highland Brigade fell – 'Scotland is poorer in men but richer in heroes' – and where, amid choking dust, a huge crowd hailed Dick Duckworth, 'one of our best men.'

A pattern was set: thousands of miles criss-crossing the country, civic welcomes, snatched sightseeing and the farewells of war cries and Auld Lang Syne. In two months the tourists played 23 matches, on hard granite, in hot choking dust, even, once, on immaculate grass – 'they even turfed the stretch in the middle of the pitch'. So that when they saw the sea again they braved the shark-fencing by diving into the warm Durban waters. And everywhere entertainment: plays, fancy dress, music halls, football on skates, Kaffir war dances, ubiquitous smokers' concerts in halls where footballs, decorated by festoons of greenery, dangled above the tables.

Everyone did a turn – Vincent Hayes earned encores by borrowing a soldier's hat to render 'Ye don't catch me on a gee-gee's back again'. And echoes of the Boer War: a match in the siege town of Ladysmith; the hundreds of British soldiers in every thousands-strong crowds; the graves of fallen soldiers by the rail track; sightseeing on Wagon Hill, where the Gordon Highlanders fell – even a glimpse of the real Spion Kop; and collecting shrapnel bullets from the battlefield. So that cartoons proclaiming 'peaceful footballers' soon celebrated Test wins by depicting hat-trick hero Billy Hibbert as sharpshooter.

They went along the coast by boat, disembarking by being 'slung over the side in baskets' onto a tug for a voyage around the bay. Their favourite trip was to Pietermaritzburg, and the magnificent scenery around the

Tugela River. They stayed in the Imperial Hotel, palm court and all, and watched ice hockey. The ground where they played in the town was the prettiest and one of the grassiest all tour, and they won 6-0.

Twenty-three matches, 23 wins, 143 goals scored. An overwhelming series of victories produced 'record gates and guarantees exceeded'. They were the best English team in 'any branch of sport' yet come. Colonel Dalrymple of the Transvaal FA praised their model of an Empire's 'sound body and mind'. He took a sideswipe at the Corinthians, such dilettante amateurs that young South Africans had taken to 'walking about sideways with feathers in their hats', in imitation of those tourists.

After years of trying they had got 'tip-top English', men to do 'men's work'. When Transvaal offered tough competition the pros reverted to type. 'They appeal automatically ... If they are bowled over in the penalty area they are more emphatic. They know the value of a little posing in a sitting posture.' England won 1-0 amid another authentic touch from home – the referee was barracked. The biggest crowds, thirteen and fifteen thousands (and over £1,000 taken – this was no sixpenny gate here – despite the stands being rushed by spectators) were at the Wanderers ground, where the English cricketers had played two Tests months earlier. Dick scored a few; dominated the midfield; fed his wingers 'perfectly', and in partnerships with Harold Fleming 'played a beautiful game, full of vigour and sting'. After winning the first two Tests he sat out the last, and was missed as they trailed twice: '[Richards] was not Duckworth, and you can well believe this.'

They played good football even in their own terms. Tourist Bob 'Golden Locks' Benson, of Sheffield United, later died during the Great War, not on the Western Front, but at Highbury as an ammunitions worker. In 1912 he reminisced about South Africa, saying he had never seen forward play in his life like the versatile Vivian Woodward displayed on that tour. The tourists fulfilled all their hosts' expectations and were recommended for a bonus on top of their £20 expenses. They were also given a cake, inscribed 'English Football Association. For their Clean, Clever Play.' They got back to wives and babies on August 20th, eleven days before the 1910-11 season started.

**1910-11**

Moral philosophy sent Dick Duckworth on his way from the Empire, and the moral philosophy of a new season welcomed him home – 'there is no game quite like football. It is full of life. It quickens the pulse and fires the imagination ... It is played by manly men, but it is an unfortunate fact that we cannot all be players. Thousands of us must be lookers-on.'

One season without a trophy left Manchester United's programme editor anxious about their prospects. He was also aware that United's infrastructure (especially with the dead hand of the Football Association's oversight upon them) did not support a serious title challenge. As late as November 22nd, 1910, the board, contemplating a daunting overdraft, decided 'to negotiate transfer of several players in view of the financial position of club'. Dick could have been forgiven feeling weary after his exhausting summer. Certainly, colleagues suffered. Vincent Hayes, so brave in forecasting a championship win on the eve of the tour, only played one first-team match on his return; and George Wall appeared to have 'left behind in South Africa his amazing celerity and much of his characteristic sparkle'. Tourists from other clubs also succumbed to injury or loss of form.

In addition, it was back to the dangers of urban life. The United party travelled from St Pancras to Plumstead for their first fixture, against Woolwich Arsenal, in a convoy of motor cars. They were delayed by burst tyres and by a collision with a lamp-post – Charlie Roberts gashed a shin, and Billy Meredith damaged a shoulder. Undeterred, virile Dick 'quickly reduced Arsenal's left wing to impotence'. He also took sustenance from 'Players' Union United's' continued resistance. At Arsenal, contrary to the authorities' wishes, they defiantly wore the union's badge on their jerseys. Cartoonists received the gesture as manna from heaven. Their theme was that encounters with fellow unionists would be gentle affairs, and those with non-union teams anything but. This was not pure fantasy: United's acrimonious battles with the likes of Blackburn last season were contrasted with their almost foul-free match with Newcastle. Billy Meredith complained that the Players' Union 'has been grotesquely distorted and maliciously misrepresented in the public press'.

However the union was now almost defeated. One element in the settlement of November 1909 was that the Football Association would repeal 'that awful bogey Rule 31' and withdraw from involvement in club/player financial relations. The clubs themselves had enjoyed the period since The Amnesty – they were now 'running on much cheaper lines' – and asserted a ready-made plan. First, and crucially, they closed the inter-league gap that the players had previously been able to exploit. The Football and Southern Leagues agreed: players could take a share of their transfer fees, under conditions; introduced some 'ungenerous bonuses'; and increased the maximum wage from £4 to £5, but in two ten-shillings increments over four years' service.

Moreover, whilst this plan would not come into effect until 1912, the clubs immediately enacted a new power that permitted them to sack a player on fourteen days' notice, for 'palpable inefficiency'. The pros were unimpressed: 'we are not within a hundred miles of a settlement of our troubles.' The new cartel took immediate effect; a player called Wood who had moved between the two leagues was left stranded – his old club wanted a transfer fee that no one would pay. The same thing happened to Charles Kingaby, a recent but unsuccessful signing by Aston Villa for £300. But he did not accept it. He sued.

The first Old Trafford derby in September 1910 was an early football highlight. Sixty thousand people, the largest crowd at that time ever to see a League game in Manchester, watched Dick Duckworth decide the outcome. His 'tremendous drive' could only be parried by City's goalkeeper, and the appropriately named 'Knocker' West followed up. United won five out of their first six games, but it was not good enough for their followers. Dick Duckworth was 'admirable', and Sandy Turnbull received a backhanded compliment: he has 'shed that pose of indifference that prejudiciously affected his play last season'. But otherwise Harold Halse, Alec Bell and newcomer 'Knocker' West were all criticised in United's own programme.

As usual their success was compared unfavourably with the wonderful autumn of 1907. Then, in the first seven matches, 21 goals had been scored and only six conceded; this year it was 13-8. Nevertheless, the team was still resilient: in October, United beat the redoubtable Newcastle 2-0, despite being reduced to ten men early on. The 1910-11 championship race settled into a three-cornered fight, between United, Sunderland and Villa, who emphasised the gap by winning 5-0 against fourth-placed Middlesbrough.

The odds against United increased. On September 30th, the FA Council had a busy meeting. They received a report on the successful South African tour, and the rehabilitated Dick was promptly chosen for his first of five appearances for the Football League.

However they also decided United's financial fate. Just as J H Davies celebrated Old Trafford's gates doubling those of Clayton's, his creative accounting was stifled. United, and not the Manchester Brewery Company, were made to take responsibility for purchasing Old Trafford's land and ground. A big hole was appearing. The club's liabilities also now included £11,344 in advances from Davies, which was in addition to the previous £7,230 discovered 'in breach of the rules'. The FA stipulated a 'proper constitution' and required United to raise alternative capital 'so that the present controlling interest of Mr Davies shall cease'. It was a recipe that brought United to the brink of liquidation twenty years later (Harrington, P 1994).

There was a final postscript of revenge: the Council gave the present FA Cup (the trophy despoiled by a copy being made for Davies) to Lord Kinnaird.

Dick took his chance: 'Dick Duckworth was able to reproduce his best club form in the Inter-League game last Saturday, and our modest right half-back is a prime favourite for the position in the International matches.' His first representative appearance echoed the imperial character of the summer exploits. He played for England versus Ireland, 'the Grand International League Match,' at Celtic Park, Belfast on October 8th, 1910.

Any Anglo-Irish contact carried political overtones. The Irish newspapers expressed anxiety, lest anglophile Association Football was falling behind nationalist Gaelic Football. The real test of quality was against the League professionals, and it was special, a rare event – only once a year did England come to Ireland. Missionary aspects were underscored by a stress on the South African veterans in the English team, like George Holley and Billy Hibbert – the 'deadliest of shootists of the South African tour'. Dick Duckworth, who 'gave many smashing good displays against the Colonials, is one of three halves who have done so much to bring Manchester United to their present foremost position, and he is to be depended upon in any emergency.'

It was the hottest ticket in town. The *Irish Athletic News* complained bitterly about their punishment for not sucking up to the officers of the Irish Football Association. The editor of a rival, brown-nosed organ occupied six prime locations whilst the *News* was allocated one solitary 'rear seat' – 'suffering, as we usually do, because of our own isolation and independent position'.

A hell indeed, but Celtic Park had an intriguing alternative name that featured in the match adverts: 'See Paradise packed for the first time.' Paradise was being built up for the season's biggest game: 'extensive banking operations had been carried out to all sides, a considerable portion of the fine trotting track was made available for spectators by bringing the palings forward, while vast improvements were carried out to the grandstand which is now an extremely handsome, commodious and well-sheltered structure.'

Dick and the League party stayed at Belfast's Grand Central Hotel. Their journey to the ground was easier than most. The demands upon the tramcar service out of the Falls Road were too great, particularly climbing the hill, and desperate measures were called for – 'thousands took a short cut through the Laundry grounds to make up for the delay, and several ladies in negotiating the barbed wire suffered in consequence.' When they arrived, the 'celestial enclosure' looked heavenly, sheltering under the hills on a glorious afternoon. 'The westering sun, as he dipped behind the shoulder of Divis, threw its brilliant rays across the ground. And right well looked the "classic slopes of Paradise".'

In contrast was the very human recklessness of an overflowing football crowd: 'it was extremely strange to find spectators taking their places on the top of the corrugated iron stand. It must be good stuff.' The English started well. The right midfield of Duckworth and Holley played a 'very strenuous game' and their 'fast work looked ominous' for the Irish. Billy Hibbert was 'fearless and keen' and fresh from a four-goal performance for Bury. His shots 'were a treat. There was some sting in them.' They took a two-goal lead, but neither reflected well on Irish goalkeeper Fred McKee, and there were mutterings in the crowd. The Irish fought back, urged on by their legendary Johnny Darling. They scored, causing dangerous celebrations and a strange interlude for Darling – 'loud and prolonged cheers, and the "unreserved" on the corrugated roof gave a few steps of an Irish jig. Dramatic pause. Telegraph boy runs across the field. Wire for the Irish captain John Darling. John reads slowly. No answer. Game proceeds.'

The English soon reasserted their spell: 'the passing of the Saxon lot was delightful. They seemed to work the ball like magic, and more than once the opposition was simply fooled.' Manchester City's James Conlin restored the two-goal lead, and all took traditional or innovative half-time sustenance: 'Bovril for the players, which was well appreciated. Bovril chocolate for the public – if you pay for it. Nevertheless, it is good value, and worth a bob a bar.' Good value. The entrance charges were nine pence, one shilling – a bob – and two shillings for the grandstand.

England took charge in the second half, the qualitative difference one familiar through the ages: 'when travelling with the ball [the Saxons] seemed to be always on top of it, whereas the home players kicked so far ahead, and were easily robbed ... Some delightful in-and-out passing preceded the fourth goal.' And a fifth and sixth. The 'jeering hostility of the crowd' turned on keeper McKee. The English missionaries went straight home after the game, but captain Colin Veitch thought McKee was harshly treated. The Irish thought Fred asked for it: 'discard every trick that savours of "swank": drop the retorts that encourage the hostile demonstration ... then the public will not regard you in a ridiculous light.'

Dick's second match for the League, on Monday, November 14th, posed a fundamental question – 'what was good football?' That same afternoon the country was asking another: what was good government? 1910 had been spent in political stalemate since January's General

Election. It had left the major parties neck and neck, with the Liberals sustained in power by coalition with the 'radicals' – the rising Labour party and Irish Nationalists, led by John 'The Dictator' Redmond, hell bent on Home Rule. The Suffragettes, maintaining an uneasy truce whilst the Women's Suffrage Bill had a chance, kept a watching brief. But radical law was not possible whilst the Tories held sway in the House of Lords. Their most famous victim, the Liberals' 1909 Budget, had provoked the last election.

In almost his last act, old King Edward had sponsored a Veto Conference, to find a compromise way forward. That this was a 'lamentable failure' was finally accepted the previous Friday, and Prime Minister Asquith visited new King George at Sandringham, in search of 'guarantees'. Asquith would not dissolve parliament unless he was assured the country's will would prevail afterwards. Only the King could guarantee this. If Asquith won an election called to limit the power of the House of Lords, would the king create enough new, sympathetic peers to ensure constitutional change?

From 3pm to nearly 5pm on November 14th, in Downing Street, the Prime Minister heard the King's reply, brought by his secretary, Lord Knollys. Another election became inevitable, but it was a tight fit to complete by Christmas. The Suffragettes ended their truce, and over a hundred were arrested for invading parliament. The Tories played subtle defence: they denied rejecting compromise, they were only defending against an extremist, over-mighty Commons. Liberals like Winston Churchill attacked the Tories for vetoing everything: 'All roads lead to Veto ... we cannot get forward.' Polling started as early as December 3rd, and concluded on December 20th. The result was almost an exact reprise of the January election. The major parties tied on 272 seats; and in England the difference was only 140,000 in over four million. But because of 74 Irish Nationals the Coalition's majority increased fractionally, from 113 to 116.

From 3pm to nearly 5pm the same glorious Monday afternoon, Dick Duckworth was up the road, at White Hart Lane, playing for The League against the Southern League. A small-but-quality crowd – 'many well known persons in the football world in the grandstand' – watched The League take complete control: 'tap, tap, tap ... oh so clever.' The contrast 'was as plain as a church steeple'. The League 'went about their work as gracefully as a 'Varsity boating crew. They pulled together ... the Southern Leaguers were like men in punts. They used the long pole.' The League's football was 'tantalisingly beautiful ... the men slipped the ball from one to the other, and they got to the goal by quick and well-timed passing.' 'Tap, tap, tap ... what a line to play for England! Our senses tickled by the finer phrases, but they didn't get goals.'

This totally dominant team was three-nil down at half-time! Billy Hibbert and his international inside-forwards, Tim Coleman (a Players' Union Outcast back in the summer of 1909) and 'Tadger' Stewart of Newcastle, were 'shockingly bad marksmen', 'almost laughably' putting shots wide or over the bar. It was curious: what was good football? The League pulled two goals back in the second half, but Dick twisted his knee badly trying to block a shot from England left-winger Bert Lipsham. Duckworth was carried off early, beginning three years of vulnerability to injuries.

Back in the League, the impenetrable goalkeeping of Middlesbrough's Tim Williamson (Dick's League teammate in Belfast) left a 'bad taste', although it was United's only defeat of the season at Old Trafford. Once more Dick was 'splendid' in winning at Preston and against Notts County, although their giant goalkeeper Iremonger prevented United winning. Manchester United won seven games in succession against their toughest competitiors, other Lancastrian clubs, until Dick was missing, partly because of tragic events in his personal life. 'Dick Duckworth has suffered a grievous loss in the death of his brother, and our popular half-back will be engaged in a mournful duty this afternoon.'

In fact, Dick missed two months of uneven results. It was his longest absence so far and he saw that the panoply of professional football continued to unfold, without him. There was a battle of the scorers, with 'Our Albert' Shepherd showing a resurgence of form with sixteen goals in two months – his ninth four-goal haul took him clear of Billy Hibbert at the top of the scoring charts. Sadly, ex-miners like Shepherd, Hibbert, Dicky Bond, Billy Meredith and Alec Downie had to play another match in aid of a mining disaster, when 350 were entombed in Bolton's Pretoria Pit (collieries were commonly named after Boer War locales).

There was also the continuing battle of professionals for status. The fashion for writing newspaper columns could be a tightrope for celebrity players. At last pro footballers could follow the example of football legislators and referees by doubling as journalists and reporting and commenting on contemporary issues. But this freedom was in tension with the still authoritarian context for football.

And one star fell off the tightrope this Christmas. Dicky Bond was the England winger who provoked a crowd riot at Sheffield back in 1906. Quick-tempered Bond was once again first choice for his country – he played in all the 1910 internationals – but after this rebellious show he did not play again. Bond was now suspended by his latest club, Bradford City, for misdemeanours and was left out against Manchester United. Authoritarian old football figures recommended even more draconian punishment, sending naughty players back to their old, pre-football jobs. That would have been hard on Bond. He had been a professional for ten years, but was criticised for not saving a thousand pounds in that time. He had started at ten shillings and sixpence a week and graduated to £4 in three years (about the time when Dick Duckworth become a pro). He had also got £150 benefit after seven years service. Bond penned a column openly critical of City's directors. Unfortunately, soon afterwards the player and the club made their peace, and City's statement said Bond was repudiating any criticism of the club. He made desperate attempts to pull the piece, but it was too late – 'Football Editor. Must cancel this week's article. Compulsory – DB.'

Then there was the latest football scandal. At last the law caught up with Colonel Poole, the power behind Middlesbrough's unscrupulous approach. The Colonel's known brinksmanship had led one former secretary to include in his contract a clause stating that any suspension by the football authorities would not affect the secretary's salary. In the run up to the Sunderland derby, Colonel Poole was promoting his candidacy in the forthcoming General Election. Middlesbrough players signed his manifesto and even canvassed for him. On match day, sandwichmen paraded the ground advertising his candidature. A win would round things off nicely. Boro's latest secretary offered Sunderland captain Charlie Thomson £30 to ensure this. Thomson reported the bribe and both Colonel Poole and the secretary were banned.

Players and officials continued their ongoing conflict. 1910-11 constituted a record for foul play and endless debates about refereeing, particularly the infuriating offside rule. The terms of the debate are very familiar: Billy Meredith complained officials were ruling against those in passive positions – 'unless the man playing the ball is taking an active part' referees should keep out of it. Even so, footballers' camaraderie often won through. Dick would have heard how the police foiled United at Christmas. Bradford City's goalie half-stopped a shot, and clawed it back from the line as United claimed a goal. The referee hesitated, glanced at his linesman who made no signal, and then received confirmation from an unexpected source – the constable on duty patrolling behind the goal: 'it wasn't through, Mr Referee, it wasn't through.' No goal, said the cop.

Injury emphasised vulnerability, and thoughts turned to the future. In January 1911 Dick Duckworth became 'mine host' of a tavern in the town. Old professionals also had to look to their laurels against young upstarts. Alec Downie at last moved on to captain Oldham's first First

League season – but not before recycling an eternal football parable. 'Telling us how in one of our matches an excited young forward challenged him to fight for £50. Alec laughed and told the pugilist he hadn't been in the game five minutes.'

United now needed a spark to set off a promising but so far unsubstantial season. The Old Trafford honeymoon was wearing thinner, as its genteel suburban atmosphere lacked the energy of gritty inner-city Clayton. Even 'wholesome and wholesale victories' could not match the raw excitement of *the* autumn of 1907. Previous wins had 'lacked the full-bloodedness of the overthrow of the Arsenal, and the enthusiasm of the spectators was in marked contrast to the classic calm that generally pervades the Old Trafford arena.'

The financial drain of the new ground also continued to restrict United's ambitions. Manchester United were not bidding for the season's big transfer target. Jock Simpson had been a Scottish star for years, but Scotland would not play him because he was born, like Dick, in Manchester. England would not pick Simpson because he was so obviously Scottish. The deal was done in London, with Sunderland, Newcastle and Everton all after him. It was not straightforward. In Liberal Britain, Simpson was thought 'quite within his rights in selling himself to the highest bidder,' yet there were rules. Simpson needed compensating for exchanging his £5 a week wage with Falkirk for the £4 maximum operating in England. He also needed to sell up his billiards saloon business. Ambitious Blackburn paid a record £1,800 transfer fee, and from the start Jock Simpson captured the public's imagination. Dick Duckworth's South African colleague, Robert Benson, was a lucky recipient – Simpson's debut at Sheffield United happened to be his benefit match and boosted the attendance to 25,000.

Nevertheless, players like Billy Meredith still felt success was not beyond United this season, and looked for reinforcements from within. 'If we can only get Dick Duckworth and Harold Halse fit again and in their best form for the second half of the season we shall still come out all right. Dick Duckworth – a man with tremendous leg muscular development – has had a very bad ankle, and it was still troubling him last week.' As always, United were ensconced in winter training quarters, at the Shakespeare Hotel, Buxton, although Meredith and most of the other lads had no need to get fit: 'we don't want training.' Which was fortunate, because breezy Buxton in the depths of winter was no place for anything except 'fresh air, heaps of snow and fun'. And the occasional special event, for example, when Dick Duckworth and George Wall were presented with their South Africa tour medals – 'handsome and of pretty design.' Wall was worried about the effect of the South African award being the thirteenth gold medal of his career, and indeed it was not a vintage year for Wall – there were no appearances for England in 1911.

Dick was immediately able to renew his telepathic relationship with Billy Meredith: 'delighted at the quick way he got into his stride. He played a beautiful game. Somehow he always seems to know what I am thinking of doing.' Dick went straight back into the big time – a 1-1 derby with Manchester City (promoted the previous season) on January 21st. The sixpenny admission generated another thousand pound gate but as usual a massive 40,000 crowd meant much fainting, crushing and worse – twelve people were seriously injured. United's critical programme editor found the famed 'midline' wanting, even though Charlie Roberts 'played on one leg practically the whole of the game', and Alec Bell's 'artful wriggling out of difficulties was positively delicious'. Dick, just back from injury, was pacing himself: 'Duckworth did not evidently feel called upon to do his utmost against a depleted wing, but the manner he reduced Jones to absolute impotence in the second half was a taste of his best quality.'

The following week United's championship challenge was on the line. Thanks to a goal by South African tourist Arthur Berry, Everton led 2-0 at half-time at Old Trafford. After the interval 'United pressed hotly, Duckworth scored with a beautiful drive into the top corner', and an equaliser followed.

Back in those autumn Inter-League games Dick was the man in possession, but now that the first England selection was imminent he had not played enough recent games. He was only just in time even to try for honours: after two months out, on the following Monday Dick played for the North in the international trial. Dick 'lived up to expectations' but was disappointed. The England selection on February 1st was met with dismay, severely condemned by the press, particularly the choice of the 'old guard', Billy Wedlock and Ben Warren at half-back. Ninety per cent of footballers were said to prefer Charlie Roberts to Wedlock, the Bristol Worrier – Roberts' neglect was one of the 'curiosities of English football'. Memory of the 1910 international was still fresh: Wedlock could neither 'feed' his forwards nor hold the formidable Scots centre-forward Jimmy Quinn.

The Scottish FA mocked: 'oh, there's no comparison. Wedlock makes the crowd laugh, but Roberts is the real goods.' The Wedlock/Roberts controversy had started five years before, when Colin Veitch withdrew from a Professionals versus Amateurs match at the last moment. The FA were impressed by Wedlock's dedication, travelling the length and breadth of the country on a Sunday, to substitute. This appeared in stark contrast to Roberts' attitude towards international recognition in 1905 and 1906, and thereafter Wedlock enjoyed the selectors' undying affection: 'I-will-never-leave-or-forsake-thee-give-me-a-lock-of-your-hair-and-your-counterfeit-presentment-that-I-may-wear-it-next-my-heart.'

Similarly, Dick Duckworth and Andrew Ducat were thought superior to Ben Warren, now playing his last international season (ending with 22 caps). The other controversy was the choice of Sheffield United's Robert Evans at outside-left instead of Georgie Wall. Billy Meredith was particularly scathing. Evans had been his colleague in the Welsh team, playing ten times, but had recently been discovered to have been born in England. Although some said Meredith was himself frustrated that he was born just a matter of yards into Wales, Evans' selection became Meredith's favourite insult.

The selectors' choices were made to seem premature following the great Cup-tie that Saturday, February 4th. The Cup continued to outstrip its previous popularity: crowds were almost forty per cent up on 1910. For the third time in six years United were drawn against Aston Villa, but now the sides were the only challengers for the League title too – 'the giants of the game were to be pitted against each other'. The victors could win the double of Cup and League. Old Trafford was a fortress: United old boys Alec Downie and Bob Bonthron had difficulty getting in, as did the Post Office Messenger Boy vital for getting accounts of the match out!

United v Villa was Old Trafford's biggest stage yet: the attendance of 65,101 was the largest for any Cup-tie other than the final, and the receipts (£2,464) were a record for a 'sixpenny gate'. 'Goodness, what a sight.' The pitch was 'shut in by three immense banks of thousands of capped and coated enthusiasts, which formed a solid mass right up to where they ended in an even, dark edge outlined against the soft grey of the winter sky.' Inevitably the younger elements of the crowd had to break into the playing area to squat around the pitch.

Dick made an early impact, forcing the ponderous Villa goalie to 'an especially good save from Duckworth, who shot with all his might from twenty yards'. Then George Wall shot in thrillingly off the underside of the bar – 'a snatch chance at fortune' – prompting the 'usual frantic hand-shaking and other wild scenes'. Villa fought 'wilder and wilder' but to no avail. Wall was like the old Wall and Dick 'was the finest half back on the field'. The two men seemed to have done enough, in the biggest club match of the season, to stake their international claims: 'one feels sure that the superb form of both George Wall and Dick Duckworth against the Villa must assuredly have secured recognition. Each revealed his finest form, besides which that of any other rival to the position appears insipid.' Ben Warren remained a 'grand old player', but now Dick Duckworth was demonstrably 'faster and cleverer than any man in his position today.'

United could taste a Cup and League double when two weeks later they went north and, in front of a 45,000 crowd, beat the champions Newcastle. Dick and his colleagues were in good spirits as they waited for their train from the north-east to their next Cup retreat in Swindon. Their paths crossed with the team from Charlie Roberts' home town, Darlington, and there was much joshing. Wouldn't it be great if we met each other in the English final? The Darlington lad, who was also captain of Manchester United, proved he was no romantic: 'Yes, wouldn't that be a good thing to us.'

There was to be no good thing for United. As in 1906, 1907 and 1908, United came up against another 'Jabberwock of the English Cup'. Another strong southern side, and United drawn away. West Ham were a successful team, unbeaten at home, and over half of them local lads. What sort of locality was that? Manchester United's programme offered two uneasy visions of the Londoners – the home of the latest 'dreadnought' battleship; or the palace of Henry VIII's Queen Anne Boleyn?

The Thames Ironworks that supplied the origins of United's latest opponents were fully committed to the battleship race with Germany, which was a constant context of Dick's football career. In March 1909 the European war nearly broke out in the same way it did in 1914. Franz Josef's Austro-Hungarian Empire annexed Bosnia and Herzegovina. Inflamed Serbia was supported by Russia until it received an ultimatum. Unlike 1914, they backed down. The near thing added to the public pressure on the British Government to build more Dreadnought battleships to match the Germans. Four? Six? The music hall refrain wanted more: 'we want eight and we won't wait.' Battleships or pensions? War preparations or social reform? These tensions produced the famous budget of 1909 and the final showdown with the House of Lords.

So what was the dominant image? The threatening European present, or the ancient connotations of the ground's name? It was history that prevailed: Manchester United were beaten 'with the sun setting over historic Boleyn Castle on that fatal Saturday afternoon'. West Ham had their own slant on tradition: 'What luck! What a draw! The best club in England ... Today is undoubtedly the most important so far in the club's history.' Yet they were not overawed: we 'can still astonish the North and the Midlands, who almost to a man are Manchester mad'.

West Ham's programme contained giveaway inserts, a recent postcard photo of Manchester United's first and second elevens, which lacked Dick Duckworth because of his injury. But Ernest Mangnall had contributed the player sketches: Dick was five foot seven and a half inches, weighed eleven stone seven pounds, and was 'a grand combination smasher'. The ground was 'packed to the utmost' despite the shilling gate. The historic 24,000 crowd contributed a very contemporary £1,698.

Interest was nationwide. Eight photographers recorded Charlie Roberts' toss up with the West Ham skipper and ubiquitous referee Bamlett and three cinematography crews were 'whirling around' throughout. It was a humid atmosphere. The huge hoardings at both ends of the ground were laden with many adventurous spirits, oblivious to 'their peril'. An athletic sailor climbed the roof of the stand, followed by a soldier, butcher and 'a little stream of nondescripts'. The ambulancemen were busier than at a Cup final, with exhaustion, accidents and assaults: 'one youth was carried out with his head swathed in bandages, struck with some missile thrown indiscriminately.'

There were clashes on the field too: George Wall and an opponent were once 'clinched so tightly' that they could not use their fists. West Ham were lucky – Manchester soon had Wall, Halse and West 'practically out of action', injuries that threw the onus on their great half-backs to save the game. 'So quick on the ball,' they went in where 'the attack was hottest'. 'Duckworth was cheered for a brilliant run along the right wing.' But United could not hold out, and there was no snow to persuade Herbert Bamlett to save them. West Ham's winner came two minutes from the end.

The selectors, ever alert to amateur talent, were impressed enough by George Webb's display against Manchester United to pick him against Scotland. The press could not believe this 'pitiable' decision: to favour this fancy goods warehouseman, with only ten goals this season, over the proven Northern pros Shepherd and Hibbert. Winger Caldwell, who scored West Ham's winner, nearly missed the quarter-final with Blackburn. He mistakenly took the fast train from Fenchurch Street, and was only able to get off at Upton Park tube station by pulling the communication cord.

United not only missed out on the Cup quarter-finals, but they lost the crowd record from the Villa tie, as a crowd of extraordinary proportions – 76,000 (receipts £2,547) – packing every nook and cranny watched Chelsea versus Swindon Town at Stamford Bridge. Even reporters left early: 'what happened subsequently I cannot say, for it was necessary to escape from the crowd in time to get away from the scenes of crush and disorder which a late phone message tells me occurred at Walham Green [later Fulham Broadway] Station.'

The championship race became a cracker. Manchester United let in two goals in the last ten minutes to draw 2-2 at Middlesbrough. Ten fixtures left, and United led Aston Villa by two points, but they had played a game more. They needed to recover momentum quickly, and Dick Duckworth's 'great shot' set United on their way to beat Preston 5-0: 'some twenty minutes had gone when Duckworth fastened on the ball in the Preston half, raced ahead in that stylish, rapid way of his, and from twenty-five yards range volleyed the ball, hip high, into the far corner of the net. In vain McBride threw himself across the goal. Helped by the wind the ball flew at an amazing pace.' Then United drew with Oldham at Old Trafford, when an injured Dick Duckworth lasted only half a game. Oldham boasted an enigmatic 'Lady' Woodger as Dick's direct opponent. Lady? The only lady Woodger could be compared to was 'a suffragette holding a couple of policemen at bay'.

The season came to its climax. When Dick was fit again, the title was on the line. Two league games to go, and United led Aston Villa by one point. Dick was thrust straight into the penultimate fixture, and possible decider, between the teams in Birmingham. 47,100 watched Aston Villa win 4-2. Now United were one point behind with one game to go, but before that Old Trafford had the honour of hosting the replayed 1911 Cup final. Newcastle had been watched by an average of over 40,000 in their six Cup matches, but the Old Trafford crowd of 56,607 was a midweek record. The Wednesday replay proved a powerful attraction:

'NOTICE TO EMPLOYEES

All requests for leave of absence on account of toothache, severe colds and minor ailments, funerals, picnics, Church socials and the like, must be handed into the head of the department before 10a.m. on the morning of Wednesday's match.'

As often the key figure, *in absentia,* was Albert Shepherd. In 1908-09 Shepherd's goals drove Newcastle to the championship. In 1910 he broke the First League scoring record and took them to the Cup final. But he nearly did not make it himself. In protest against barracking by the home fans he walked off the pitch. The FA disapproved. A committee led by J J Bentley considered suspending Shepherd from the final, but instead deprived him of his rightful place as England's centre-forward against Scotland, and fined Newcastle. Shepherd's two goals had won the 1910 final and his eight goals steered Newcastle to the 1911 final against

Bradford City. But on Good Friday Shepherd tore ligaments in a collision, and he was never the same again. The new Cup, made by Fattorini and Sons of Bradford, therefore stayed in the city of its manufacture.

So to the last matches. Manchester United were at home to third-placed Sunderland and needed to win: Villa were at Liverpool, where a draw would be enough. United started badly. Another of his South African colleagues, George Holley, put Sunderland ahead, but Dick threw himself into the thick of the battle: 'Duckworth was the man of a fine line of middle men.' It was cold, wet and wretched. Reports varied about whether there were five or twelve thousands in 'sodden' Old Trafford to see the championship decider. Nevertheless, the enthusiasm was 'unbounded' as United overhauled Sunderland to win 5-1. Their involvement was enhanced by the score in the Villa match (where the Anfield crowd was 25,000) being regularly updated in chalk at the boundary edge. At the end Dick also waited at the edge of the field to see the final result – Liverpool 3, Aston Villa 1.

To celebrate the championship, Dick Duckworth and his United colleagues had an outing by motor to Chester races. It would be 41 years before the title was won again, but a tradition was established that was last repeated in May 2003.

Care for a chocolate? Manchester United defied the authorities by wearing their Players' Union badges in September 1910. The press reaction – imagining how union brotherhood threatened competitive sports – enraged Billy Meredith

Scottish hero. Dick Duckworth's most dangerous opponent against the Scottish League – 'Oor Jimmy' Quinn

**P(L)AY UP, SUNDERLAND.**

Taking Toll. [Bottom] Manchester United took toll of champions Sunderland in Dick Duckworth's last autumn. [Top] but could they beat bogey team Middlesbrough and climb to the top of the pile?

**A First Offender.**

First Offence? When Kingaby, on behalf of all professionals, made a legal challenge to Aston Villa, and by implication all clubs, over the validity of its employment contract, football presented itself as all innocence

CHAPTER EIGHT

# 1911-14
# TOWARDS THE PRECIPICE

The next two seasons were ultimately frustrating, but in each case Dick always had a chance. The First League was once more very competitive and Manchester United were one of many clubs close to the honours.

## 1911-12

1911 was the first autumn in five years that United were not consistently among the First Division leaders. In a September home draw with Sunderland, Dick's 'pace and craft were good to see', and there was the usual hard battle with Sheffield Wednesday, 20,000 at Old Trafford seeing a 3-1 win – 'some delightful scuffles were going on between Robertson and Duckworth. At first the half-back usually won, but Geordie put in an oar now and then.' Dick also started a well-constructed goal: 'Duckworth had snapped up a pass of Campbell's, and he put the ball to West, who spun it out to Meredith. I do not know any other outside right who could have taken the pass, for the screw on the ball was remarkable, but Meredith kicked it dead, ran on, stopped and ran on again, absolutely baffling McSkimming. Then the Welshman centred to Turnbull, who twisted round as Spoors went for him, and transferred the ball to West. West put it back to Halse who was quite uncovered, and a grand shot left Davison helpless.'

United were again defeated at home by Middlesbrough, and led Liverpool into the last fifteen minutes, and lost. Was the edge off United's motivation? Some critics said they sat on leads, others that they started slowly and tried to make late comebacks. Their programme noticed the players had been around a while: Alec Bell was rivalling Billy Meredith in the Perpetual Juvenile Stakes. Georgie Wall pushed the going rate for a benefit up to £750 in a home defeat to Tottenham in November:

'If points were distributed for superiority in controlling the ball so as to bewilder an opponent for the moment, instead of driving it into the net the greatest number of times, then Tottenham would have returned empty-handed. The United were often prominent with the touches many spectators quite erroneously regard as the cream of football, but they carried their so-called cleverness too far, and found, when it was too late, that they could not net whenever they liked – an idea some of the players seemed to hold until near the end.'

Dick Duckworth was still playing in 'capital style', impressing for the Football League in October. Dick 'gave the best display' beating the Southern League 2-1; a week later saw a 4-0 win against the Irish League. This season's showdown with Aston Villa was different, as both 'Real Champions' were in mid-table: 'two fine teams fiercely contesting every yard of the playing space, furious play from first to last, much skill, great vigour, and complete proof of a keen feeling of rivalry.' United's defenders foiled Villa, but if 'none of these three were on the spot, Duckworth was sure to turn up as though he had dropped from the clouds.'

Dick was now 'a local worthy' who debated high theory with United's programme editor. Who was a right-half's primary responsibility, the opposing winger or inside-forward? Dick favoured taking the inside man, and noted that that was how United played in the 'glorious year' of 1907-08. True, answered the Editor, but that was when United had quick backs: now they had slower ones. They also had bad knees. Since United had upgraded on the tough Scot, Bob Bonthron, their backs had been fragile. Burgess, Holden, Hofton: all winners, all international class, none played much. Resources became threadbare. Dick now needed to drop from the clouds a lot.

Reserve Oscar Linkson was a pick-up from the 1908 Continental tour but he was now front-line defence at First League leaders Newcastle in December. Dick had to play 'a clever and cautious game', protecting Oscar and preserving an otherwise impressive 3-2 win. Against Bolton, watched by 35,000, his 'remarkable powers of recovery … gave Linkson, who was none too safe, admirable protection. Linkson fell in every imaginable position.' To stay in contention Manchester United needed Dick in 'international form, and he has even outshone his midline colleagues' as they took eleven points from six games, and reached second place.

Newcastle could respond to setbacks. They beat the transfer record again, by paying £1,950 for Billy Hibbert. Hibbert was 'loath to leave Gigg Lane', but £450 from the fee and a gold watch as a memento from Bury overcame initial reluctance. The deal was done Thursday evening, but Hibbert did not sign until he played a last Bury game, against Manchester United and his old South African comrade Dick Duckworth, that Saturday afternoon.

United's setback came on Christmas Day 1911 – a 0-1 home loss to Bradford City. It was a most 'piquant match', and a typical holiday scene. 'Among the frolics' was the sole score, an own goal by Duckworth. The crowd itself provided others. During the half-time interval, sandwichmen paraded around the perimeter with boards advertising local pantomimes and other attractions. The crowd made its own entertainment by throwing coppers at the luckless ad men. When the teams came back there were attempts to clear the ground of coins. Bradford City goalie Martin Spendthrift, *aka* Spendiff, was quicker than most, gathering up as many coppers as within his vicinity. Spendiff had no pocket for his bounty, so he placed his collection behind one of the goalposts. The game resumed, and United pressed forward. A ball flew across the goalmouth and Spendiff went down amongst the boots. He lay still, a few yards out, unable to safeguard his treasure: 'this was just the chance that a youngster had been waiting for. He jumped over the railings, crept on hands and knees, and "pinched" Martin's coppers from behind the post.' The Old Trafford crowd roared and clapped. Spendiff was 'chafed' by fellow players but thankfully saw the joke himself.

George Wall was 'chafed' for other reasons. His teammates started calling him 'Jack Johnson' after the then World Heavyweight Boxing Champion. Wall earned his title when he took exception to a spectator's filthy language at Goodison Park and went into the crowd. There was much sympathy and little criticism for the combatant: 'little wonder that even quiet-mannered Georgie wanted to have a go.' *The Liverpool Echo* however tracked down the offending and offended fan:

'Just before the interval Roberts fouled an Everton player, and I hooted him and cried, "Play the game." A few seconds afterwards a spectator pointed out to me that Wall was jeering at me and pulling faces. I saw this, and also saw him deliberately kicking mud towards me. He came over the touchline and threatened to throw some mud at me. I dared him to do it. He said, "Shall I see you after the match?" I replied that fighting was not in my line. The linesman attempted to get him on the field of play, but before he could persuade him he hit me over the eye, and the mark of his muddy hand was left on my eye. I retaliated.'

Wall did not let it bother him, and scored the next week. A Wall goal was usually an inspiring event: 'in 19 cases out of 20 if Georgie Wall gets a goal it is a double-barrelled, jewelled, half-minted thriller ... nearly broke the net.' This time it inspired no one: not a desultory 8,000 Old Trafford crowd and not a team both Charlie Roberts and Billy Meredith reckoned had gone stale. Even the terms of praise were now tinged with the sense of a passing era: 'Duckworth is a rare player. Next to Roberts, Bell appealed to me as a tactician. These three men will live in football history as masters of the ball and intelligent in all they attempt.'

United went on their winter sojourn, this time to their 'favourite training ground' on the north-east coast at Whitley Bay, either side of playing

Sunderland on January 27th. It was not a happy stay. The team had lost their way and Dick had to sit through a lecture 'on the duties of a narf back' by a club director. It was an important match: both clubs were on 26 points and needed a winning run to get among the leaders. Dick was 'the best of the halves' on turf in a terrible state from heavy rain and snow. The star was another old South African tourist. George Holley, sometimes criticised for 'his impersonation of a spinning top', had a career-high match. His four goals in a 5-0 thrashing of United included one where he 'twice cleverly tricked opponents' (probably including Dick) before unleashing a terrific shot for his hat-trick – 'undoubtedly one of the finest goals this season'. United's league challenge was ended, and the sense of a tiring team was palpable: 'there was a time when Manchester United could plough through mud and keep up a great pace in heavy going.' George Holley's performance got him back on the international scene after a two-year absence, whereas Dick had played under a considerable handicap, as Billy Meredith reported: 'Dick Duckworth, by the way, was really ill last weekend. He got such a cold at Whitley Bay that to relieve his chest on Saturday morning he was making himself vomit. He was simply reeking with cold, and looked only fit for bed, but he played, and jolly well.'

Dick also made his last challenge for an England place, representing the North in the international trial. His prospects were enhanced when Ben Warren had a mental breakdown. Dick and Everton's Harry Makepeace 'are without doubt the fastest and best English-born wing half backs playing in the league today.' Dick *was* selected alongside Makepeace, but for the English League. For the England internationals the right-half place went to his contemporary, Tom Brittleton. The Wednesday man had also been waiting in the wings during Warren's reign, and battled Dick in many clashes over the years.

So Dick Duckworth received his most important representative honour, equal to the minor England games against Wales and Ireland. He played for the English League against the Scottish League at Middlesbrough on February 17th, 1912. The night before, the teams went to the theatre fraternally together, whilst the authorities met conspiratorially. It was a scary moment for football, not seriously repeated until the Bosman ruling nearly a century later. The transfer system, basis of the players-as-commodities structure of professional football, was under threat: 'abolish the transfer and the game will be split right down to its foundations.' The pace of Kingaby's case against Aston Villa's retain-and-transfer powers was quickening. That Friday in the High Court the Lord Chief Justice himself heard his barrister's application. "'I will ask that your Lordship will try this case. It is a football club case." [Laughter] Lord Alverstone replied "I certainly can't promise that. I know nothing about that." [Laughter].'

With the mice away at the theatre, the fat cats of the Big Three – Football League, Scottish League and Southern League – spent four hours honing their strategy: how to respond if transfers were declared illegal; and how to further strengthen their cartel, to produce even more 'uniformity of rules and management'. Ironically, Dick's theatre companions included James Fay, who took over the Players' Union from Manchester United and ran it for forty years in the wake of Kingaby's case being lost.

Dick played in front of the full England defence (Williamson, Crompton and Pennington). Fay replaced the injured Harry Makepeace and charismatic Tom Boyle was centre-half: he had the 'artistry of a Japanese juggler in his toes', and was 'as irresponsible as a lady who pines for the franchise'. Up front were some of the country's brightest forwards, and one, fed judiciously by Dick, became a star: he 'never played a finer game'. Charles Buchan. Tall and just twenty – recently signed by Sunderland for £1200 – Buchan charmed all, and especially the Scots who swore his classic style revealed Scottish blood. The English saw him as a reincarnated 'hammer of the Scots', the 'new Bloomer'. He also emulated his namesake's longevity by establishing Arsenal's dynasty in the late 1920s.

Their most famous opponent was the legendary Scottish centre-forward James Quinn of Celtic. Since coming to pre-eminence in the 1899 Scottish Cup final, Quinn's talent had been formidable, his temperature explosive and his bravery extraordinary: 1912 was to see his last, eleventh international. But a terrible series of injuries had also caused him to miss more. He only played this spring's England game after suffering badly against Ireland: stud marks on his eyebrow, a lacerated lip, black and blue legs, several bruised ribs, but he still beat them. For the League, Crompton and Pennington remembered the way Quinn destroyed them in the 1909 international. They were so wary of his propensity to pounce on 'scientific clearances' that they gave away corners when he was five yards away.

With Quinn kept at a safe distance, Duckworth and Buchan took charge, playing brilliant football in front of a 25,000 crowd (producing a record League international gate of £930). They won 2-0, their only victory over the Scottish League between 1908 and 1915. It was the last of Dick Duckworth's five appearances for the English League – at the time only a dozen players had made more. Dick had done his duty: 'the way the English eleven triumphed was most satisfying to those whose breasts swell with patriotism.'

The Cup was Manchester United's remaining target for 1912: and it was as much financial as football. Cup gates were up twenty per cent, even on 1911. The military portents of time-running-out continued to intrude into football's world. The big Stamford Bridge Cup crowd included many sailors, and you know what sailors are: 'delightful little incident just before the match, a couple of sailors of the Royal Navy dashing out from the crowd, clambering up one goal, and tying on the crossbar something like a doll, decorated in the Chelsea colours.' United won 5-1 at Coventry on a bright, frosty day and then as usual drew Aston Villa. But unexpectedly, Villa lost a replay to obscure Southern Leaguers Reading.

United had had too many losses against southern opposition to feel comfortable. They changed quarters again, to the even more-convivial-than-usual surroundings of Ascot. In contrast, Reading's total weekly wage bill, trainer included, was just £43. It was a day of days for the 'clean southern town', 'such a constellation of football stars has rarely been seen in conjunction.' United hired a special saloon carriage for their brief train journey, and lunched at the Queen's Hotel. Reading was invaded by a 'locust swarm' of supporters and peddlers. One approached some unrecognised United players to sell rosettes: 'Good old Reading: United 'ill be fairly down the hatchway'. When appraised of his mistake, unabashed he 'pulled from another pocket a batch of "red" favours "all the way from Manchester this morning".' Watching with detached amusement, 'the great Meredith lounged against the hotel door ...'

The crush was so great that the corporation banned vehicles near Elm Park. The police duly halted United's convoy, despite manager Mangnall's fervent protests: 'our cabs were stopped and the visiting team had to walk the last 200 yards to the ground.' Reading's last big day was in 1901, when a record £906 paid to see Spurs. Their 1911-12 league gates averaged just over £100. Now 24,069 created a new record – £1,350. £1,151 was paid in silver, and when it was piled on the counting table Reading's directors 'danced for joy'.

After five minutes, United's goalkeeper Hugh Edmonds acted the country yokel in 'one of the funniest things in football'. An indirect free-kick was given against him for carrying the ball, and their captain quickly briefed his defenders on the meaning of 'indirect'. 'Roberts told all his men the law, with the exception of the goalkeeper.' Edmonds promptly spilled the shot into his goal: 'to say some of the Manchester players were astonished would be to put the thing very mildly, and for a time they appeared to be overwhelmed by such an extraordinary mistake.' The great half-back trio, perhaps showing the first signs of wear, raised their game: 'at times from what I have heard – not from what I have seen – I have been inclined to wonder whether the old line of Duckworth, Roberts and Bell was quite as good as it used to be. But I have no doubt now that it is as clever as ever when the occasion demands. Nothing could have been finer than their work when once they have recovered from the shock of that wonderful goal ... with an outstanding degree of cleverness, they combined an irresistible dash.' The replay provided Reading with further 'undreamt riches' – 29,811 paid £1,051. United won 3-0.

Nevertheless the league failures – five games for just one point since New Year's Day – were having a debilitating effect on receipts. United's next home win attracted only ten thousand, which meant a gate of £250, nowhere near enough to stem the albatross of debt United had accepted with Old Trafford. The players got anxious: 'they are paying off The Money They Owe [emphasis in the original] out of every league gate by an arrangement with the contractors ... there are only four home games left.' However United made £5,000 on the 1912 Cup campaign, thanks to the kind of big pay day now coming. For Cup opponents Blackburn had gone from strength to strength and were now the likely champions. Manchester United took the opportunity to double admission prices for their quarter-final. Billy Meredith brushed off the consequent 'grumbles and talks about boycotting'.

There were a lot of grumbles during the current month-long miners' strike that jeopardised all of industry. Everything depended on coal: money was short; jobs went; trains stopped. It was the wrong time to double prices. Nevertheless, Meredith reckoned the place would be packed, and he was right: 'at the present time the nation is unfortunately plunged into the midst of the most devastating industrial war that has ever been known, and yet 59,300 folks assembled at Manchester and paid £3,114 5s.'

If United's directors (and contractors) were gratified by a record gate, the Rovers had freer ambitions. Unbeaten for three months, three points top of the league maybe, and they had never won the championship. Yet they wanted to regain the Cup, which they had won more times (five) than anyone else – but not since 1891.

The match was worthy: 'one of the best Cup-ties I have seen.' At first Rovers were being 'wiped out in very summary fashion'. The masterful United half-backs set up a lead: 'I must confess I do not know exactly what happened' – an own goal. Shots and centres bombarded Rovers' goal, but then Jock Simpson squeezed the ball passed United's keeper. A goal was certain until from out of nowhere appeared full-back Oscar

Linkson – 'another roll would have done it.' 'Duckworth, Roberts and Bell were again a great power' and had Simpson in 'almost complete subjugation'. Almost. United's lead was only one goal. Simpson got free once, and Wattie Aitkenhead headed the equaliser amid great United protests. The players got very excited and the play hotter and hotter, but no more goals.

Nevertheless, United's tie took second place to a four-match saga that was the footballing highlight of 1912. The all-Yorkshire clash between the 1911 Cup holders Bradford City and the losing finalists in 1910, Second Division Barnsley, was not just about football. It also captured the spirit of the miners in the midst of an epic coal strike. The first match contributed a record £2,000 gate. Another tremendous crowd gathered at Valley Parade, and the legend of the striking South Yorkshire miners tramping over the Moors to follow their champions was established.

The second replay was at Leeds and once again the miners walked west. This time a little detail like paying was no obstacle. Although, truth to tell, after three weeks without pay that was no little detail. The first gates were rushed, and taken, at noon, and the ground filled up. The penniless wasted no sympathy on the many five-shilling ticket-holders who queued but never got in. Some went further and robbed turnstiles of £100. Mounted policemen, with foot reinforcements, gradually cleared the playing pitch until, bang went another gate, and another two thousand flooded in. The referee battled the 'mob-rule' until three minutes from time, and then abandoned the match. Nevertheless, when rumours spread *half an hour later* that the referee would complete the last three minutes the 'crowd poured pell-mell' back in. Officially the crowd was 45,000 and £1,800 was taken.

Bradford wanted the third replay at Old Trafford: Barnsley, conscious that would overtax even their supporters' feet and stamina, argued for Sheffield. Another 38,241 paid £1,500 – altogether the tie generated over £6,000 out of penniless strikers and those put out of work by the strike. Three matches, not a single goal. When Barnsley equalised in the last minute, a fifth tie loomed, to be held goodness knows where. It ended Bradford City's truly impressive record – twelve consecutive Cup-ties without conceding a goal. Their spell was broken. In the dying seconds Barnsley scored again. It was enough: the Cup holders were out and the miners went on to win the Cup.

Understandable then, that professional spectators like The Veteran were jaded for the United v Rovers replay: 'it is perhaps possible to see too much of big football, for watching in six days four important matches – three of them attended by over 130,000 people, and in the other the crowd broke in – makes one pause and ponder over what a great hold the game has obtained upon the public, and become a little weary of all the bustle and excitement. You can have too much of a good thing.'

Double prices were no disincentive in Blackburn. There were chaotic scenes on Monday night, as 5,000 tickets quickly went to those at the front of the long queues – some folk buying as many as 150 sixpenny tickets for their work-mates in the surrounding mills. 39,286 paid £2,110. If the appetite of tired journalists was sated, this 'extraordinary Cup-tie' was the perfect antidote: 'the ground was packed to excess, and the vast majority of the spectators were raised from the depths of despair to a delirium of joy. In all my experience I do not think I have seen a wilder scene of enthusiasm than when the Rovers scored the equalising goal five minutes from the finish.'

Earlier, United had taken what seemed an unshakeable hold – 'they played as if the game was over.' They took an early 2-0 lead: Duckworth, Roberts and Bell were proving a 'rare trio' and Roberts in particular – 'never has he played better in attack or defence.' They stayed comfortable until deep into the second period ... deceptively comfortable: 'that was when Manchester United made a fatal mistake, and it is one they are rather prone to, and have more than once been warned about.' Jock Simpson's goal was lucky. Charlie Roberts thought it from an impossible position, but it was deflected in a unstoppable parabola into the goal.

It was a rude awakening, and United found it difficult to recover the initiative. Nevertheless, six minutes to go, Dick Duckworth gave Billy Meredith the ball. He centred and either Turnbull or West seemed certain to score, until the burly Crompton rushed over and 'bowled both of them over'. The ball went to the other end, and United's goalkeeper and full-back Stacey were shepherding the ball over the goal-line until Simpson got between them, 'hooked it over their heads' and Aitkenhead headed in. 'A shocking mix up.'

Rovers were fresher in extra-time, and their centre-forward rushed through the middle. Stacey went to him, was brushed aside and fell heavily. Then the Blackburn forward, defender Linkson and goalkeeper all collided in a heap: 'and then the ball was seen to be rolling slowly – oh, so slowly – towards the goal. There was not another player within thirty yards, and the crowd almost held its breath as they watched that rolling ball. It meant so much, and there was a yell of joy as it just crossed the line without sufficient impulse to roll a yard inside.'

Charlie Roberts was the nearest defender and noted once again the forces of law and order working to forestall United – 'a policeman near to goal waved his helmet to help it on its course.' Roberts was too late:

'the policeman went nearly mad with delight while I stood looking at him.' Rovers had won 3-2.

It was a harsh lesson: United were the cleverer team, 'but cleverness is not everything, and too much confidence is sometimes fatal.' The enormous crowd included an England sporting legend who was wrestling with uncomfortable feelings. Jack Sharp was a Liverpool sports outfitter who was about to join Everton's board of directors. He had impressive credentials: twelve years an amateur right-winger with Everton, a Cup winner in 1906, a loser in the 1907 final, five times in the top three between 1902-1909; twice an England football international, and a Test cricketer as well. Sharp was a passenger in a car *en route* to the Rovers v United replay when it passed through Ormskirk at midday. John Wallace, twelve years old and son of a horse breaker, had just been let out of school and was kicking a tennis ball with his pals. A kick sent the ball out of the back lane into the main road. The boys chased after the ball, Wallace just ahead, when Sharp's car came along, travelling about 'seven or eight miles an hour'. Wallace ducked, the car hit his head and ran over him. He suffered terrible injuries, and was dead on arrival at Ormskirk Cottage Hospital. Two other lads had close escapes. After a hour's upsetting delay the footballing party continued on its way to Blackburn and the match which ended Dick's season.

United players were tortured by 'The Tragedy of Blackburn': 'if ever players were sick of being asked "How did it happen?" the Manchester United men were on Thursday night, and, to put the lid on it, I was awakened at seven on Friday morning by two workmen discussing the match in another room. As I opened my eyes one was saying to the other – "They say these chaps were leading two goals at half time." "Yes" I groaned, and said things.' Even a week later others were still saying things, less charitable things: 'do you know, Mr Editor, it is actually a fact that there have been people trying to spread the lie that Manchester United Did Not Try at Blackburn in the cup tie? Could anything be more uncalled for, less deserved, or more wicked? I think not. Let me tell my readers that Manchester United pulled their souls out to win at Ewood.'

The season was not quite dead. In Billy Meredith's weekly column he and Dick Duckworth had a bit of fun when the FA's Rules Revision Committee recommended changing the offside rule. A declining Newcastle were relying more and more on Billy McCracken's offside trap. Manchester United had come across it themselves, and Charlie Roberts commented: 'if both sides played it, the game would be ruined.' The Rules Committee recommended that offside should only apply between the respective penalty areas (extended right across the pitch) and the goals. Billy and Dick had not laughed so much in years. Billy Meredith of course was still thinking of Evans the Welsh Englishman when he mocked the proposed change: 'as a football joke it should be classed with the playing of Evans in English international matches.' Meredith fancied he could play another eighteen years under that regime (he nearly did anyway) but for wing halves the likely extra work would cause them to strike, or change position, as Dick Duckworth preferred: 'when they pass that, Bill, I shall retire if I can't play outside right.' The offside rule change was not accepted.

**THE SUMMER OF 1912**

This time there was no celebratory club outing. The players dispersed: Dick Duckworth was glimpsed in June in a shooting lodge, whilst colleague James Turnbull went off on his honeymoon, and disaster – somehow he lost his FA Charity Shield medal. By a strange coincidence his namesake lost the FA Cup medal he won with Manchester City in 1904: 'footballing burglars are on the increase ... Alex Turnbull, who is fond of stealing goals, has had his house ransacked.' Dick Duckworth had his own lost-medal story. His medal went missing in one of his licensed premises in the late 1920s and was found, and returned to him twenty years later. It was later given by his daughter to the Manchester United Museum.

In 1912 there was already widespread interest in the historical dimensions of football: not only in the recollections of the past and judging the present in terms of the past, but in speculating about the future. One clairvoyant was George Robey, music hall artiste *par excellence*, would-be serious footballer, and Dick Duckworth's host in various post-Cup final celebrations in 1909. Robey's prophecy of football's place in the world of 2000 was almost spot on: 'football will be the one topic of conversation, the one business by which fortunes are made, and the one great link which will bind us to the old days of slavery.'

Robey saw that the relentless increase in football crowds would end in worldwide competition that demanded the participation and attention of vast numbers of the world's population, but not that footballers would benefit from this popularity. He wrote when the Players' Union had clearly failed to change their conditions of employment, but when top players either received more generous benefits, or a significant share of their transfer fee. But, although writing in the days before the European states carelessly tossed away vast numbers of young men as cannon fodder in the Great War, before the rise of Stalin and communism and Hitler and fascism, Robey saw the footballers of 2000 as the pawns of totalitarianism. His metaphor however was one commonly used in this Golden Age: football as spectacle, as bull-fight, as gladiators.

Robey imagines himself falling asleep and awakening in 2000. His old haunt, the Oxford Music Hall, had been demolished to make way for a vast football stadium, like the millennium Old Trafford. He did not see Chelsea, Spurs or Arsenal surviving until 2000: rather the model of the future was Manchester.

This vast stadium belonged to *London United* and there was a game on: 'a quarter of a million inside, each paying a sovereign – "phew, a quid for a football match" – for the game against St Petersburg Athletic … Huge covered-in structure which is surrounded by a high grille … My first impression is that I am here to see an exhibition of wild animals … "Why, man alive, the players would escape if there was nothing to keep them in. Jackson, our centre-forward, got smuggled away to Tokio, where he was to play for the Tokio Wanderers, under another name … They had a Japanese warship up the Thames to carry him off, and they bribed him with the promise of a packet of cigarettes every week … [Then followed] the entrance into the arena of the players, who are chained together like a gang of convicts".' The players are freed, temporarily, from their shackles by an armed referee. London United win the game by the only goal scored by a recent capture from the Columbus Corinthians. The footballers get no reward: 'they catch the players when they are young … Government officers searching for abandoned children, who are trained at the proper national football nurseries.'

The crowds take pity, like the onlookers of a Roman amphitheatre, and throw on tiny wedges, 'small pieces of tobacco, which are highly prized by the men.' Robey the groupie asks if he can see the players before they leave. 'Leave, leave where?' The players were kept in a compound, a concentration camp within the stadium, guarded by armed sentries. He saw them anyway, whilst they were being 'rubbed down' prior to their meal of raw steak, brown bread and water. Then early to bed, prior to the midweek match with Madagascar. This would attract an audience of half a million, with 'special one-day aeroplane excursions from Africa, India, Australia and in fact, from all over the world.' On his way home, Robey sees an unruly procession of armed guards dragging a prisoner, whose 'lagging footsteps are being hastened by an occasional lash from a long whip. "And the man's crime?" "Found with incriminating documents upon him, which show he is implicated in a scheme for smuggling Hyde Park Rangers' goalkeeper away to Siam. It's certain hanging for him".'

So George Robey's millennium Public Enemy No 1 was the Football Agent. Then again, they hadn't thought of an England manager in 1912.

**1912-13**

The new season started disastrously for one of Dick's England rivals. Andrew Ducat broke his leg in September. He was taken by horse ambulance to hospital, and spent the rest of the season on sticks. His career seemed over at 26, but extraordinarily Ducat came back, playing football three times for England after the Great War, and cricket for England against Australia in 1921. He later dropped dead at the crease in a match at The Oval.

Professional footballers were under increasing pressure from crowds, clubs and the football authorities. Observers thought barracking was getting worse: 'the tendency to decry the efforts of players seems to be more in evidence this season than ever.' Goalkeeper Billy Scott was suspended by Sunderland after missing training to visit his ill mother. Soon after complaining about being the victim of persistent crowd hostility, he was sacked for 'palpable inefficiency'. Everton suspended teenager Tom Browell, who had been signed for £1,550 on the strength of being the best England centre-forward of the century, but months later he was suspended *sine die* by his club – accused variously of either betting on goals or disobeying training orders. Chris Buckley (briefly Dick's teammate for United in 1907, and for the English League in November 1910) was suspended for two seasons for failing to substantiate his claims that Aston Villa had offered him a £250 illegal financial incentive.

Meanwhile the Players' Union were losing more Workman's Compensation cases. Irish international Bill Renneville sued Aston Villa after he jumped to head the ball, and injured his right knee, causing fluid. Case dismissed. He had not proved 'at all that anything in the nature of an accident took place'. More fundamentally they lost the landmark case which really mattered, Kingaby's suit against the retain and transfer system that held footballers to one employer, indefinitely. It was a body blow. The Union struggled to pay the costs, and the football authorities put the boot in – refusing permission for a benefit match to boost union funds.

The financial pressures on Manchester United had another tangible effect: manager Ernest Mangnall went off to Manchester City. Billy Meredith managed both to praise Mangnall's ability to run United as cheaply as possible and to comment sourly that he would no doubt enjoy 'an advance of his already handsome salary'. Worse, by the time United had their new manager (none other than J J Bentley, who had barely retained his FA and League offices in United's 1909-10 financial scandal), City beat United and headed the early League table. Manchester United and Sunderland (without a win in their first five matches) were among the stragglers, but it would be their duel in the underbelly of the League that would determine the 1912-13 championship.

The League thus echoed the slide towards war in Europe. It was not the overt rivalry between France, Germany and Great Britain that mattered – it was events in the underbelly. In 1912 Turkey was under pressure from all sides: Italy attacked, the Albanian Moslems rebelled, and the Christian states of the Balkans conspired. In October and November these allies – Bulgaria, Serbia and Greece – forced Turkish armies back almost to the gates of Constantinople. But they also set a slow-burning match to the powder-barrels of Europe, because behind the strife of these local forces stood the vital interests of the Great Powers.

Also in November, Sunderland beat Manchester United 3-1 without the help of their tormenter last season: George Holley was absent, grieving the death of an infant daughter. Soon another defeat on a foggy November afternoon left United in semi-darkness in more ways than one, down in fourteenth place. But it remained a competitive league and both Sunderland and Manchester United could still mount a challenge. Dick Duckworth gave United momentum by meeting another crisis at full-back, although he had been 'too clever a half back for too long now to be a big kicking defender.'

As on previous occasions Dick 'came out of a trying ordeal with colours flying.' United beat Liverpool 3-1, and Sunderland kickstarted their own season by winning 7-1, although they were still down in twelfth position. Both kept going: Sunderland won 4-0 and 4-1; and United 4-0 and 3-1, before beating Chelsea twice over Christmas, 4-1 and 4-2. Finally Dick won his last derby – 38,223 added £1,142 to City's coffers, although as usual an overflowing crowd interrupted play. Manchester United's coffers were not as deep as their players' quality: they 'have a conception of Association football unequalled by any other set of men'. To ask City's young defenders to face the mature skills of Dick Duckworth, Billy Meredith and Sandy Turnbull 'was akin to asking a ploughman with slow and cumbrous feet to outwit three trained sprinters in a race'. It was an old story, but not one destined to be repeated: 'United played as they liked with fine combination and calculation.'

Manchester United next faced the new leaders WBA in another Battle of the Giants. United reaffirmed their reputation as a side that gives the opposition a goal start, and then claws it back. The match 'deserves to become historic', not least because the 27,000 brave souls on a rainy January day were inspired to shed their suburban reticence: 'never in the history of the game has a team made a greater effort to circumvent heartrending ill-fortune ... The spirit of their superb struggle permeated and influenced everybody present, and converted a usually chilly spectorate into a solid body of loudly demonstrative partisans.'

'Herculean' Charlie Roberts led the way. A goal, and a man, down at half-time, he famously told his team that they might as well lose by three as by one, and 'attack should be their only object'. More, if the others would not score, he would. And lo and behold Dick hit the crossbar and Roberts headed an equaliser six minutes from time. 'Dick Duckworth played one of the finest games of his career, and I am curious to know where he and the rest of the old brigade, who were supposed to be approaching the sere and yellow, have unearthed the secret of perpetual youthfulness ... the "old uns" outraced, outpointed, outvigoured their opponents at every stage of the game, and ultimately played them to a standstill.'

United went undefeated in ten games and Dick was in 'international form', but the penultimate disappointments of his football career were at hand. They lost 1-4 at Everton amid a deluge of illness and injuries: United were reduced to nine men if you count a concussed Dick Duckworth who 'was dazed for thirty minutes from a blow on the head and knew little of the closing stages of the contest'.

Now United needed to beat the latest leaders. Sheffield Wednesday were three points clear of several other clubs, and five points ahead of United. 38,000 watched a tough battle: there were 'frequent breaches of the law' (although Dick himself was 'very fair') and the referee was popular with nobody. Both players and crowd grew 'vastly excited ... when Wall started to argue with Mr Bollimer very volubly we looked like having a scene, but fortunately for himself Wall calmed down'. United scored twice in two minutes, held firm, and won 2-0. The championship was once more as tight as could be.

In the Cup, United reached Plymouth. Argyle's victory in the previous round found the ears of the FA Council: 'most unscrupulous,' 'unsportsmanlike.' Preston had been left 'terribly sore' and 'scarred'. J J Bentley confirmed United too had heard the news: 'our fellows have received heaps of papers and letters about it, but they simply laughed at them.'

It had been raining for days, and went on raining. The rain spoilt the gate, but still 20,717 paid £827 to get very wet. They included United's usual travelling hundreds, carrying their 'bells and rattles' and 'red and white sunshades'. They also showed the west country that the polluted air of 'Manchester had not spoiled their lungs'. Mancunian exiles in Plymouth found a new voice: 'last time you was cheerin' Argyle: "ay lad, but Preston wasn't t'United".' A 'wild man with spectacles' was unacceptably unsure of his allegiance, waiting an hour to 'mildly ask as the teams came out "And which is the Argyle team?" *Which is the Argyle team!'* Such lack of commitment was out of place: 'cold print will never do justice to that shout. Did the ancients tell us not to shout before victory? But then the ancients had no English cup-ties.'

Argyle feared United's stars: 'where's Meredith? was the prevailing query, and there was great anxiety to see Turnbull.' George Wall set up the opening goal and scored a second after running from halfway. 'Brilliant' Dick was the 'best half-back on the field', but afterwards 'Duckworth, thinking he was diving into a well filled bath, went head first into one that was nearly empty. He sustained slight concussion.' Two concussions in a fortnight. Dick was so 'ill that he was put to bed at an hotel, and a medical gentleman summoned.' Each club took £365 from the match.

But he was back for the following week's 'Battle Royal' at Ewood Park where a huge crowd produced receipts of £1,050. Blackburn were still buying the best: West Ham's Danny Shea came for £2,000 (he was reckoned to pocket £600-£700 himself) to partner Jock Simpson on the right flank. Together, they cost £1,000 more than the whole of the United team: the millstone of Old Trafford was exerting an increasing effect. It was a tough game, and Dick was hard-pressed by Rovers' new flier. A month later Joe Hodkinson would be preferred to Georgie Wall on England's left wing, and against United he showed 'magnificent pace, superb stride, strength of purpose. That he did not produce a goal was due to brilliant defence, Duckworth sticking grimly to his fleetfooted opponent.' Then thirty thousand saw United beat Derby 4-0. Dick 'tackled and fed finely', so little was seen of the great Steve Bloomer. Now in his twenty-first season, scorer of 350 League goals, it was Bloomer's only appearance at Old Trafford.

United's third round match, against championship rivals Oldham, represented another major challenge for professional football. The sport, and industry, had taken a serious blow. Manchester City versus Sunderland seemed just another chaotic big-time Cup-tie. Officially 41,709 paid £1,566, beating the attendance record that United had established only a month before. But there were 60,000 inside Hyde Road: Sunderland's centre-forward Richardson, separated from his teammates, only played by 'climbing over the hoardings'. They were twelve deep all round the pitch. Sunderland led 2-0 when something different, and potentially destabilising happened. City supporters took calculated action to stop the match. The Union's Players' Magazine explained: 'quietly, the hundreds standing inside the barrier in front of the grandstand moved forward half a dozen steps over the touchline. Appeal and expostulation was alike in vain. There was no excitement, no disorder. With magnificent affrontery, the 'wreckers' stood about in groups idly chatting, or cooly surveying the scene'. The referee succumbed to the inevitable, abandoned the match, and 'the crowd quietly dispersed, cynically indifferent, quietly contented'.

What had happened? Was it part of a wider willingness by groups to challenge the accepted order? Young men, like those invading football grounds, were reacting violently to the continued suffragette agitation. During this month in London alone, angry mobs were regularly breaking up suffragette meetings, outside Holloway Prison, in Hyde Park, down Regent Street. On Wimbledon Common speeches were interrupted by chants and motor horns, before a large band of young men rushed the platform, overpowered police, wrested the suffragettes' tricolour and then threateningly surrounded a house in which the women had taken refuge.

Or was it simply a failure of sport, a home crowd being unable to take a beating? Or the effect of an evil that had been a developing threat throughout Dick Duckworth's career – gambling? The Football Association promoted parliamentary bills, and prosecuted those who tried to bribe an England player. Professionals, moralists, the football establishment all lamented the effects, but widespread disapproval made little difference: 'this betting craze has come to stay, and no amount of press criticism can stamp it out.' What was subsequently accepted as the 'football pools' was, before the Great War, an illegal, undercover and international affair. The means were the same: the 'abominable coupons are a curse to the game'. If so, another riot could easily happen in Oldham, as there were 'very few spectators who visited Boundary Park but had their "bobs" on'.

And if that was true for the ordinary match, so much more so for the extraordinary: Oldham Athletic versus Manchester United, the featured tie and the biggest in Oldham's short history – 'never a match down for decision at Boundary Park has provoked the interest of that due to be played tomorrow'. It was a 'battle of giants'. Both were in form – United had lost only one of seventeen games – and both were still in with a chance of the championship title. Oldham were one of four leaders on 33 points; and Manchester United one of three chasers on 32. And the Cup was something else again. Something worth putting up the admission charge for, to a shilling – no one could object, not when it was to avoid a repetition of the 'fiasco' at Hyde Road – and also worth changing the geography of the ground – Oldham erected a new uncovered stand on flat land just for this match: 'a large amount of tipping of ashes for banking purposes has been done on the banking at each end, and the club are inviting the free tipping of good clean ashes.'

Both sides had spent weeks being 'pampered' by the seaside, but Athletic returned nearer home. Their players prepared: each morning was spent in exercises, then Monday – Turkish baths; Tuesday – a stroll over the hills, then tea in town, then an evening at the Grand Theatre; Wednesday – a train to walk on Saddleworth Moor, then tea, then evening at the picture house; Thursday – a theatre evening in Manchester; Friday – 'quietly spent in readiness for the great tussle.' The barriers were strengthened, three miles of terracing stretched around the goals. They expected 50,000. United were at Norbreck, but Sandy Turnbull was sent home with neuralgia. He had three teeth extracted, and he was not fit for the match. Likewise, Oldham's George Hunter was 'laid up with a swollen face', but he played anyway 'in utter disregard of his doctor's orders, for he had been forbidden to play'.

The directors were rewarded with a record £1,496 gate, but press warnings about the small ground and the shilling gate policy served to keep the crowd down to disappointing proportions – 27,000, no threat to the 35,473 record. Manchester United arrived by car and, when Dick and his teammates inspected the ground at 2.30, they found the turf so black and bare that the tracks of their boots could clearly be seen.

The mascots paraded. Oldham's young goat pulled a blue and white carriage. When it rested the United fans jeered: 'it's taken the defeat lying down.' When it rose just as suddenly, Athletic supporters raised a great counter cheer. Manchester responded with a boy dressed in United colours bearing aloft a model of the Cup. By these measures the authorities were trying to counter the independent practice of 'fervid parents placing tiny boys in the club's colours behind the goals ... The idea has nothing to commend it save excessive partisanship, but even that has to be curbed in such circumstances.' Replica shirts, 1912.

The Oldham crowd would not be passive, and implored the band to play the latest 'rag time' favourites. It was fine weather, with a cool breeze. A host of photographers welcomed the teams. As so often for top United games, referee Tom Campbell took charge. Some of the newly erected barricades gave way, but the displaced crowd did not encroach. Dick was a 'rare breaker-up' as the two sets of half-backs cancelled each other out. Manchester United's programme later praised Dick's offensive attitude, but hinted at a neglect of defensive duties: 'Duckworth was the best half in the attack, and he provided heaps of chances for the men in front, even at the frequent risk of forgetting his duty to the forwards of the other side.' Dick's late free-kick caused the worst trouble. Oldham's goalkeeper saved, and 'Knocker' West charged him over without ceremony. The Athletic defenders reacted, 'anxious to join in the argument in a way which is not allowed on the football field.' Hugh Moffat, Dick's opposite number, dashed at the United player and would have hit him but … 'The crowd hooted lustily: "send him off".' Referee Campbell, never far away when there were signs of trouble, 'soothed ruffled feelings' with a quiet word.

The crowd at Old Trafford for Wednesday afternoon's replay – Dick's last English Cup match – was 31,180 (£1,863) and was 'treated to an explosion of hard, keen football'. Play was 'fast and furious', with United playing the more controlled football. Heavy rain fell and soon afterwards Oldham went ahead: Joseph Donnachie made a fine run and produced a beautiful centre for a header home – 'a great goal!' United besieged Oldham's goal and played 'with great dash'. West equalised. Oldham regained and kept the lead, although Georgie Wall had a last chance to equalise again … but lobbed over an open goal. 'Lady' Woodger was the mastermind of the Athletic attack, 'evolving all manner of elusive tactics,' and winger Donnachie's form earned him a place for Scotland against England. Together they were 'very cunning in their general manipulation of the ball'. Dick was playing in front of a back who was 'far too often beaten' and as a result adopted 'highly reprehensible tactics'. With Hodge in 'a constant state of uneasiness', Dick had two men's work to do, and it was too much.

Oldham won 2-1, and cinema film of the match was played afternoons and evenings at the town's Empire Theatre for the rest of the week. Influential people were also watching: the selectors chose 'Lady' Woodger for his sole England cap. Two months later Charlie Roberts played his last match for Manchester United against Oldham. The crowd was just 6,000. It was the day of a Cup final that neither side reached. The Crystal Palace saw a new record (121,919) and gate (£9,250) that prompted many to think 'it will pay them to construct an up-to-date ground'. Wembley was on its way.

There was one final consequence. That spring saw Dick's last chance of a home international. When the England team against Wales was announced, there was a change at right-half. No Tom Brittleton, but no Dick either. Hugh Moffat of Oldham played his only international. It was a last laugh, for Moffat had been in Burnley's 1909 Cup team when the wicked referee decided – Stop the Game, it's Snowing.

As in previous seasons, the Cup exit effectively ended United's season, although fleetingly there was still a chance of a third championship in six years. On March 1st, the Saturday after the bruising replay with Oldham, they were sixth, but only one point behind the new leaders Sunderland. However, United suffered the effects of the midweek Cup-tie, and lost at home 2-3 to Middlesbrough: the half-backs were slow and the forwards lifeless.

Dick Duckworth would not give up. United next went to Nottingham and beat Notts County 2-1. The home team were on their way to relegation but their legendary 6ft 5in goalkeeper Iremonger cared no less: disgusted when the winning goal was allowed he declined to return the ball for the kick off. Referee Fowler blew his whistle several times 'and motioned to Iremonger to throw the ball, but he stood immovable'. Eventually another County player got it, and Iremonger was reported for 'insubordination'.

The championship was still possible. Manchester United were fifth, only two points behind, but on March 15th their remaining title hopes went 'well, to pieces', well beaten, 1-3, at home to Sunderland. This was Dick's last appearance – injury finished his season. Sunderland were the eventual champions, by four points, four points they took off Manchester United.

There were worse things than losing a football match, a Cup, a League title. James Blair was an old protagonist of Dick Duckworth's during his time with Woolwich Arsenal, Bradford City and Manchester City – his battle with Billy Meredith was a highlight of the 1908 derby, but he was disciplined the following year for demanding a bonus in the Cup. But by mid-March 1913 he was playing with Stockport, and like Duckworth, his season was over. Blair returned to his Dumfries home in bad health, despondent that he could not play for his club over Easter, and two weeks later he was found dead in the bathroom, his throat cut.

## The Cat and Mouse Summer of 1913

The suffragette campaign became more and more militant. Just as Dick's football season ended, the arson attacks mounted: on churches, country houses and sporting facilities – a period of direct action that culminated in Emily Davison being killed by the King's horse on Derby Day. Left behind at the firesites were the messages, 'Votes for Women' and 'Stop torturing our comrades in prison'. The torture was the forced feeding of hunger-striking suffragette prisoners, but then the authorities thought of something else. The prisoners would be released when dangerously weak, but could be rearrested when they had recovered. It was called the Cat and Mouse Act.

United's great half-back line had brought the club 'fame and renown'. Now approaching ten years' service, they all wanted a second benefit.

United thought they could manage without: their young replacements had secured fourth place in 1912-13. Alec Bell went first, to a Blackburn team amongst the favourites for the 1914 championship. He kept half the £1,000 transfer fee. Charlie Roberts was offered a two-year agreement with a promise to consider a second benefit, but no 'legal guarantee'. United lamented the split in muted tones of self-justification – they were generous – but preferred to give first benefits. A disillusioned Charlie Roberts was still there for United's final trial, but resigned the captaincy: 'of course, had he been a member of the team, Duckworth would have been the new captain but he has not yet signed.'

Unlike Roberts, Dick had not signed on for the 1913-14 season. He too was holding out for a guaranteed second benefit. However, United's programme credited him with standing out 'for sound principle, but he did not make the mistake of taking up an irreconcilable attitude'. His football worth was proven: he may have missed the end of the season 'owing to a series of injuries, and there was ample testimony early in the season, that Richard D. was able to reproduce his very best form whenever the occasion called for'.

A week before the season began, Charlie Roberts was whisked away to Oldham for the record fee for a defender – £1,500-£1,750. United's final trial revealed an unconvincing side lacking gravitas and urgency: 'the old forward line ... were not quite so keen as the youngsters, and were only anxious to get themselves more fit.' The club suffered an angry response followed Roberts' departure, 'consisting merely of abuse, and suggesting such utter nonsense as a boycott.' United needed a healing gesture, and Dick Duckworth represented a potential symbol of reconciliation. However if Roberts was Hercules, Dick's behaviour recalled the characteristics of another hero: 'Duckworth is still taking the part of Achilles, sulking in his tent.'

Influential supporters expressed their anxiety by pursuing 'the possibility of fixing up with one of the most genuine players who ever stepped on a football field, Dick Duckworth'. It was a widespread response. One correspondent, from a 'large engineering firm' testified to the general feeling that 'this man should be immediately approached with reference to signing on. Public feeling is somewhat against the directorate, and unless action is taken to strengthen and maintain the prestige of the club, it inevitably means a decline in gate receipts'. J J Bentley took the hint and 'was holding persuasive conferences with Duckworth in all sorts of strange corners – I believe the first was in the dark on the bowling green ... I do not know the terms but I could give a guess that the agreement is for more than one year'. Which proved to be a very wise precaution.

Next day saw United's final trial and afterwards the prodigal son returned: now United's longest serving player by far, Dick Duckworth was made joint captain with George 'Kicks like a good Mule' Stacey.

**1913-14**

As usual the season started on September 1st exactly. A Monday. Two of the usual suspects for honours – Blackburn and Newcastle – clashed at Ewood Park. It was a chaotic start for all concerned. Newcastle set off at 10.30am, but missed a connection and had to charter their own special train. Reporters had to hire a 'four-wheeler' to make the 5.40pm kick off. The real crowd did not arrive until work finished: 'thousands of mill workers went straight from their looms to the Ewood turnstiles at 6pm.' Rovers' 3-0 win demonstrated they would be the team to beat this season.

Dick showed there were no half measures about his renewed embrace of the United cause. It was going to be a tough start, against two of the previous season's top three. They won them both. Confident Wednesday inaugurated their fine new stand, and renamed the ground Hillsborough. Wednesday had led the First Division into April 1913 until frustrated by a Charles Buchan-inspired Sunderland. A new season, new hope and new disappointment: Dick's United won 3-1. The champions, Sunderland, then found their star inside-forwards Buchan and Holley no match for United's 'great trio' of half-backs – Dick, Arthur Whalley and Michael Hamill – and were also beaten 3-1. Duckworth 'did not play like a man with a grievance, but quite in his old and best style'. Ironically, both Whalley and Hamill would both, like their predecessors, leave United prematurely, because the club would not provide written guarantees of a benefit.

Football's popularity was reaching new heights: 65,000 at Stamford Bridge for Chelsea v Spurs; Roker Park attracted an unprecedented 44,000 against Newcastle; and another record 38,000 to Burnley on a Monday evening. Danny Shea scored four goals for Blackburn as they swamped Liverpool 6-2 in their second match. Who could stop them? Not Sunderland, Newcastle or Sheffield Wednesday. Manchester United?

Perhaps not, for they suffered a lapse. Bolton's Ted Vizard was 'a perfect box of tricks, a wizard with the ball' and ran rings round United's back. Dick at first took the inside man, probably mistakenly: 'a man of Duckworth's experience would probably have had the best chance of checking the best forward on the field.' But when Dick moved out wide, the only goal followed his foul on the great left-winger. Manchester United were 'knocked off their game and converted into a worried, much-upset and over-anxious eleven'.

It was the only blemish of the glorious autumn of Dick's career, and he set them on their way at Chelsea: 'Duckworth waltzed around Sharp ... whipped in a good centre which Anderson had nothing to do but slip into the net.' 40,000 saw Dick's last match at Stamford Bridge: starting with that glorious Good Friday in 1906 when United battled to beat the Londoners to a promotion place; continuing through First Division fixtures and two Charity Shield United wins. The 2-0 win preserved his unbeaten record: 'a brilliant and beautifully balanced team ... wonderfully one-sided ... The Manchester half-backs were far too quick in their tackling, and also went for the ball with a vigour that utterly upset the Chelsea line. Duckworth, Whalley and Hamill were a complete success. They fed with rare judgement, and kept the ball low with studious care.'

Another Danny Shea hat-trick in Blackburn's 6-0 win demonstrated United would do well to match Rovers' pace: Rovers had now won all five matches, scoring twenty goals. Even J J Bentley acknowledged their 'super-championship form'. United could afford no slip-ups, and a serious banana skin loomed. Charlie Roberts brought his Oldham team to Old Trafford, and got a 'thorough thrashing'. There were 55,000 in Old Trafford. Roberts received a great reception and seemed all 'bottled up' with the emotion of the occasion. Manchester United's new 'grand half-backs turned the tide of the match', and Oldham were 'put to complete rout', 4-1. United's 'convincingly powerful display' promised much: 'the team should do big things before the end of April.' The first goal came when 'Duckworth advancing behind the Manchester right wing, lifted the ball into the goalmouth and Matthews running out utterly misjudged it in the sun ... Anderson breasted the sphere into the net.'

It was a great day for Dick Duckworth at Old Trafford, against the Charlie Roberts whom he faced in his first match for Manchester United almost ten years before. But the old timers were running on borrowed time: Steve Bloomer was not in the Derby side and even goalie Tim Williamson was dropped by Middlesbrough.

Manchester United were now credited with being the only club which could stop Blackburn running away with the championship in the way United had in 1907. Dick, a survivor of that great team, was at the heart of their resistance: 'Duckworth of course has rarely been anything less than the most dependable England right half-back for the last six years, and his recent exhibitions have been equal to the best he has ever given.' United felt that London's national papers were neglecting these fine performances in favour of the current flavour of the month, Blackburn Rovers: 'the football provided by the home eleven at Warwick Road has never been excelled anywhere, or rarely equalled, and if the players belonged to some organisations there would be paragraphs daily eulogising the swiftness of movement and skilfulness of the men in red.'

'Much feeling and bad temper' then characterised their next match – Tottenham Hotspur 'charge and charge unfairly far too often, and whenever the whistle goes against them, they assail the referee'. United showed a gallant spirit to battle through in disheartening conditions: they were a Harry Middlemiss goal down at half-time and had two men 'badly injured about the face'. Still they fought Spurs to a 'standstill', 3-1: 'the crowd cheered itself hoarse, handkerchiefs and hats went all round the packed terraces, and on the big stand there was a great display of handshaking. It's a long time since there was such intense enthusiasm at Old Trafford.'

Whenever United went to Burnley that 'snowstorm incident' in the dramatic 1909 Cup-tie 'always crops up'. Burnley were said to desire a 'healing process', to 'let the dead past bury the dead'. However the Manchester press followed United's 'gross, unworthy and above all ungenerous slander': 'let the Burnley spectators applaud their own players as much as they like, but pray let us be spared the foul-mouthed abuse of the United team, and the clamour of the crowd urging the Burnley team to resort to unprintable atrocities.'

The Lancastrians anticipated only that 'a few irresponsible youths may, when opportunity offers, indulge in a little banter at the expense of the Manchester players'. Burnley were a strong side, destined to win the season's English Cup, but Dick's was stronger – 'United have a jolly good team and need fear little'. Another 30,000 crowd watched Dick Duckworth – 'much has been written of the Manchester United half-backs of late and that praise has been richly deserved' – lead another big win. 'Burnley lost to adversaries who are well endowed with skill, weight and pace, and gave one of the best exhibitions that has been seen in the English League for some time … The half-backs were tireless and clever and … I should award the palm to Duckworth, because there was so much "old head" about all he did.'

Football was increasingly popular. For the first time, United's first four games averaged £1,000 each. Manchester City made over £5,000 profit in 1912-13. More people watched Burnley's first four home matches than the whole season twelve years previously. Individually, top players could benefit: Billy Meredith's benefit totalled £1,343, and Dick Duckworth's wisdom in negotiating a two-year contract – subject to a world war breaking out – seemed well-founded. Footballers still fared badly in the courts. Ernest Hodgkinson sued Sunderland, and was awarded fourteen shillings a week. When hurt, he had been earning £2 4s. Sunderland admitted liability but not Hodgkinson's desire for £1 a week: they argued for seven or eight shillings because he could still find other employment. The judge agreed: 'the boy must make a bona-fide effort to get work. If he does not the 14s. will be reduced.' Manchester United's shareholders delivered a vote of thanks to the players for their top-of-the-table performances. But they would not be top again for decades.

So Dick came to his last full League game, against Preston, and 35,000 watched, even though North End were bottom of the First League. 'The United were a great side.' Preston were outclassed, 3-0, by a 'splendid half-back line'. Their 'inferiority, amounting to a revelation of completely different class, proved too conspicuous. The waves of the sea do not more easily demolish a sand castle than Manchester's superb defence overrode the hazy schemes of advancement.'

United were now putting the pressure on Blackburn, who drew at home to let United move within a point of the lead: 'slowly but surely creeping nearer the head of the league … For consistency, there has been nothing to beat Manchester United.' Dick had now stepped up to replace Charlie Roberts as the inspirational and experienced leader driving United forward: 'Duckworth is playing as well as ever he did, and is well in front of his form of last season.'

Dick's last full game coincided with the worst mining disaster of the era, a fire in the Universal Colliery, Senghenydd in the Rhonda – 435 miners died, 800 children lost their fathers. Like many pits, its districts recalled an old imperial war: Ladysmith, Kimberley, Mafeking. It would take seven months to recover all the bodies.

Dick received another injury on a Monday afternoon only two days after the Preston match, in a Lancashire Cup-tie. It seemed no more than a temporary set-back, but the report carried an unintended but prophetic finality: Duckworth 'sprained a muscle of the thigh, and left the field to know the game no more'.

At first United pressed on and when Blackburn faltered, they went top, briefly. But their rhythm was disturbed, and when Dick returned on November 15th it was in the wake of three defeats in a week. The damage was self-inflicted. The previous Saturday Aston Villa had beaten United 3-1 after Michael Hamill was sent off, then on the Monday Manchester City won the Lancashire Cup semi-final. No sooner had this minor derby finished than United got on the boat train for Ireland – a sea voyage and three changes of quarters in 48 hours. They played Bradford City in Belfast: each team had signed a player from the city and this friendly was part of the deal. The ground was bad but the two First Leaguers fought out a real match: it always was when medals (worth £2 10s) were at stake. So Manchester United returned to Old Trafford tired out, to face Middlesbrough who had won in Manchester for each of the last three years.

The final circumstance for United's 0-1 home defeat was the further 'accident' to Dick: 'Duckworth got hurt, and seemed to be badly injured. He was carried off, but returned in a few minutes … meeting with another injury, was carried off again and did not return.' Until that moment Dick's Manchester United was holding its own – in the match, in the season, and in the first era of living with the Old Trafford debt. Afterwards? 'Duckworth did well up to his accident but with his retirement, the whole back division went wrong.'

In his scarred last three seasons, 1911-14, Dick's 59 League games yielded 70 points: in the 55 he missed Manchester United gained only 49 points. Without him United declined rapidly. By spring they were only one place above the relegation positions. Blackburn Rovers won the title. Manchester United won nothing else for decades.

On the first football day of 1914, Dick played his last match, for the reserves at Old Trafford. United's first team were losing 1-6 at Bolton. If he had played, Dick would have marked the new Wanderers' dangerman, Joe Smith, inside-left to Ted Vizard – together, already the League's most deadly left-sided attack. Joe scored four goals. Perhaps J J Bentley and the directors sensed the team's new vulnerability and tried to rush Dick's return. In any event, he was lost after only twenty minutes; 'the United officials made a big mistake including Duckworth, for he was obviously unfit, and carried off in great pain.'

In August 1914 the judgement on Dick's prospects carried a double meaning in both sporting and military contexts: 'it is not likely that Richard Duckworth will see a deal of active service. His knee, I understand, still troubles him.' For that same month, the Balkan powder keg exploded into the Great War. Football saw its season through, although the insults got nastier and nastier. Players went into the Forces. George Wall joined the Black Watch, survived and played on – his last game was in 1924 for Manchester's Ship Canal team. Sandy Turnbull, who shared many winter quarters with Dick, was killed at Arras with the Manchester Regiment. Oscar Linkson, whom Dick once protected so assiduously, also died in France.

As did thousands of young men who watched Dick Duckworth's matches in a decade of The Golden Age of professional football.

Before and After the War. [Top] Imminent disaster was apparent on Saturday, 15th November 1913, the last authentic appearance of Dick Duckworth, United hero. [Bottom] Charlie Wallace (pictured), along with Duckworth and Charlie Buchan, made up the League's right wing against the Scots in 1912. Unlike Duckworth, they played on into the 1920s

# Bibliography


Bentley, J J — 'The Growth of Modern Football,' 1905, p.11-14, in Leatherdale, C, *The Book of Football: a Complete History and Record of the Association and Rugby Games, 1905-06,'* Desert Island Books, Westcliff-on-Sea, Essex, 1997.

Cawley, S, and James, G — *The Pride of Manchester: a history of the Manchester derby matches,'* ACL Colour Print and Polar Publishing, Leicester, 1991.

Dobbs, B — *Edwardians at Play, 1890-1914*, Pelham, London, 1973.

Green, G — *There's Only One United*, Hodder and Stoughton, London, 1978.

Hamann, B — *Hitler's Vienna: A Dictator's Apprenticeship*, Oxford UP, Oxford, 1999.

Harding, J — F*or the Good of the Game: the official history of the Professional Footballers' Association*, Robson Books, 1991.

Harding, J — *Football Wizard: The Billy Meredith Story*, Robson Books, 1991.

Harrington, P — *The Gibson Guarantee: The Saving of Manchester United, 1931-1951*, Imago, 1994.

Kelly, S — *Back Page United: a century of newspaper coverage of Manchester United*, Queen Anne Press, London, 1994.

Wagstaffe-Simmons, G — *Tottenham Hotspur Football Club: its birth and progress, 1882-1946*, Tottenham Hotspur Football and Athletic Co Ltd; Tottenham, 1947.

FOOTBALL CLUB OFFICIAL PROGRAMMES

The Albion News and Official Programme, Villa News and Record; Manchester United Official Football Programme; The Cottagers Journal; Tottenham Hotspur Football and Athletic Co Ltd Official Programmes; Official Programme of the West Ham United Football Company.

NEWSPAPER REFERENCES

*The Athletic News; Birmingham Evening Dispatch Sporting Buff; The Birmingham Sunday Mail; Blackburn Times: Blackburn Weekly Telegraph; Bolton Evening News; Bolton Football Post; Bradford Daily Argus: Bury Times; Cape Times,*

*Capetown; Midland Daily Telegraph, Coventry; Cricket and Football Field, Bolton; Daily Chronicle; Daily Citizen; Daily Dispatch; Daily Express; Daily Graphic; Daily Mail; Daily Mirror; Daily Sport; The Evening Chronicle, Newcastle-upon-Tyne; The Football Argus, Bradford; Football Chat and Athletic World; The Football Chronicle, Reading; Football Echo and Sporting Gazette, Southampton; Football and Sports Special, Saturday Sports edition of Yorkshire Telegraph and Star, Sheffield* [until 1907]*; The Football Echo, Sunderland; Football Express, Derby; Football Herald, Plymouth; The Football Mail, Portsmouth; The Football News, Nottingham; The Football Post, Nottingham; Football Pink, Swindon; Grimsby Sporting Echo; Ireland's Saturday Night, Belfast; Irish Athletic News, Belfast; Lancashire Daily Post; Liverpool Echo; Liverpool Football Echo; Liverpool Daily Post; London Football News; Manchester Evening Chronicle; Manchester Evening News; Manchester Guardian; Morning Leader; The Morning Post; Northern Weekly Leader, Newcastle-upon-Tyne; North Eastern Daily Gazette, Middlesbrough; The Northern Athlete, Newcastle-upon-Tyne; Northern Daily Mail, Hartlepool; The Northern Daily Telegraph, Blackburn; North Mail; Oldham Evening Chronicle; The People; The Players' Union's Magazine; The Picture Post; Rand Daily Mail, Johannesburg; The Referee; Saturday Football Telegraph, Grimsby; Sport Set, London; The Sporting Mail, Birmingham; Sporting Chronicle: The Sports Argus, Birmingham; Sports Mail, Hull; The Staffordshire Sentinel; The Sunday Chronicle, Manchester; Thomson's Weekly News; The Tottenham and Edmonton Weekly Herald; The Umpire; The Week and Sports Special, Saturday Sports edition of Yorkshire Telegraph and Star, Sheffield* [from 1907]*; The Weekly Dispatch; Weekly Mercury, Birmingham; Yorkshire Sports, Bradford; Yorkshire Telegraph and Star.*

# INDEX & GLOSSARY

## OF PERSONALITIES FEATURED